D0853731

Holy Women

Holy Women

POPE BENEDICT XVI

Our Sunday Visitor Publishing Division
Our Sunday Visitor, Inc.
Huntington, Indiana 46750

The Scripture citations contained in this work are taken from the *Catholic Edition of the Revised Standard Version of the Bible* (RSV), copyright © 1965 and 1966 by the Division of Christian Education of the National Council of the Churches of Christ in the United States of America. Used by permission. All rights reserved.

Copyright © 2011 by Libreria Editrice Vaticana

Copyright © 2011 by Our Sunday Visitor Publishing Division
Our Sunday Visitor, Inc. Published 2011.

16 15 14 13 12 11   2 3 4 5 6 7 8 9

ISBN 978-1-61278-510-3 (Inventory No. T1214)
LCCN: 2011930588

Interior design by M. Urgo
Cover design by Lindsey Riesen

Cover art: *St. Gertrude the Great
Carrying the Sacred Heart of Jesus* (oil on canvas),
by Spanish School (17th century),
Monasterio de Santa Maria de San Salvador,
Canas, Spain / The Bridgeman Art Library

PRINTED IN THE UNITED STATES OF AMERICA

TABLE OF CONTENTS

CHAPTER ONE

St. Hildegard of Bingen

Her Life[1]

In 1988, on the occasion of the Marian Year, Bl. John Paul II wrote an Apostolic Letter entitled *Mulieris Dignitatem* on the precious role that women have played and play in the life of the Church. "The Church," one reads in it, "gives thanks for all the manifestations of the *feminine* 'genius' which have appeared in the course of history, in the midst of all peoples and nations; she gives thanks for all the charisms that the Holy Spirit distributes to women in the history of the People of God, for all the victories which she owes to their faith, hope, and charity: she gives thanks for all the fruits of feminine holiness" (n. 31).

Various female figures stand out for the holiness of their lives and the wealth of their teaching even in those centuries of history that we usually call the Middle Ages. Today I would like to begin to present one of them to you: St. Hildegard of Bingen, who lived in Germany in the

---

[1] Editor's Note: The material in this book is derived from catecheses given by Pope Benedict XVI during his weekly general audiences from September 1, 2010, to April 6, 2011. The texts have been edited only slightly to facilitate presentation in book form. The date each address was originally presented is annotated in the footnotes. This first entry is Pope Benedict XVI, General Audience, September 1, 2010.

twelfth century. She was born in 1098, probably at Bermersheim, Rhineland, not far from Alzey, and died in 1179 at the age of 81, in spite of having always been in poor health. Hildegard belonged to a large noble family and her parents dedicated her to God from birth for his service. At the age of eight she was offered for the religious state (in accordance with the Rule of St. Benedict, chapter 59), and, to ensure that she received an appropriate human and Christian formation, she was entrusted to the care of the consecrated widow Uda of Gölklheim and then to Jutta of Spanheim who had taken the veil at the Benedictine Monastery of St. Disibodenberg. A small cloistered women's monastery was developing there that followed the Rule of St. Benedict. Hildegard was clothed by Bishop Otto of Bamberg, and in 1136, upon the death of Mother Jutta who had become the community *magistra* (Prioress), the sisters chose Hildegard to succeed her. She fulfilled this office making the most of her gifts as a woman of culture and of lofty spirituality, capable of dealing competently with the organizational aspects of cloistered life.

A few years later, partly because of the increasing number of young women who were knocking at the monastery door, Hildegard broke away from the dominating male monastery of St. Disibodenburg with her community, taking it to Bingen, calling it after St. Rupert, and here she spent the rest of her days. Her manner of exercising the ministry of authority is an example for every religious community: she inspired holy emulation in the practice of good to such an extent that, as time was to tell, both the mother and her daughters competed in mutual esteem and in serving each other.

During the years when she was superior of the Monastery of St. Disibodenberg, Hildegard began to dictate the mystical visions that she had been receiving for some time to the monk Volmar, her spiritual director, and to Richardis di Strade, her secretary, a sister of whom she was very fond. As always happens in the life of true mystics, Hildegard too wanted to put herself under the authority of wise people to discern the origin of her visions, fearing that they were the product of illusions and did not come from God. She thus turned to a person who was most highly esteemed in the Church in those times: St. Bernard of Clairvaux. He calmed and encouraged Hildegard. However, in 1147 she received a further, very important approval. Pope Eugene III, who was presiding at a Synod in Trier, read a text dictated by Hildegard presented to him by Archbishop Henry of Mainz. The Pope authorized the mystic to write down her visions and to speak in public. From that moment Hildegard's spiritual prestige continued to grow so that her contemporaries called her the "Teutonic prophetess." This, dear friends, is the seal of an authentic experience of the Holy Spirit, the source of every charism: the person endowed with supernatural gifts never boasts of them, never flaunts them and, above all, shows complete obedience to the ecclesial authority. Every gift bestowed

The person endowed with supernatural gifts never boasts of them, never flaunts them and, above all, shows complete obedience to the ecclesial authority.

by the Holy Spirit, is in fact intended for the edification of the Church, and the Church, through her Pastors, recognizes its authenticity.

This great woman, this "prophetess," also speaks with great timeliness to us today, with her courageous ability to discern the signs of the times, her love for creation, her medicine, her poetry, her music, which today has been reconstructed, her love for Christ and for his Church, which was suffering in that period too, wounded also in that time by the sins of both priests and lay people, and far better loved as the Body of Christ. Thus St. Hildegard speaks to us.

Her Writings [2]

St. Hildegard of Bingen, an important female figure of the Middle Ages, was distinguished for her spiritual wisdom and the holiness of her life. Hildegard's mystical visions resemble those of the Old Testament prophets: expressing herself in the cultural and religious categories of her time, she interpreted the Sacred Scriptures in the light of God, applying them to the various circumstances of life. Thus all those who heard her felt the need to live a consistent and committed Christian lifestyle. In a letter to St. Bernard, the mystic from the Rhineland confesses: "The vision fascinates my whole being: I do not see with the eyes of the body but it appears to me in the spirit of the mysteries.... I recognize the deep meaning of what is expounded on

---

[2] Pope Benedict XVI, General Audience, September 8, 2010.

in the Psalter, in the Gospels, and in other books, which have been shown to me in the vision. This vision burns like a flame in my breast and in my soul and teaches me to understand the text profoundly" (*Epistolarium pars prima I-XC: CCCM* 91).

Hildegard's mystical visions have a rich theological content. They refer to the principal events of salvation history, and use a language for the most part poetic and symbolic. For example, in her best-known work entitled *Scivias,* that is, "You know the ways," she sums up in thirty-five visions the events of the history of salvation from the creation of the world to the end of time. With the characteristic traits of feminine sensitivity, Hildegard develops at the very heart of her work the theme of the mysterious marriage between God and humanity that is brought about in the Incarnation. On the tree of the Cross take place the nuptials of the Son of God with the Church, his Bride, filled with grace and the ability to give new children to God, in the love of the Holy Spirit (cf. *Visio tertia: PL* 197, 453c).

From these brief references we already see that theology too can receive a special contribution from women because they are able to talk about God and the mysteries of faith using their own particular intelligence and sensitivity. I therefore encourage all those who carry out this service to do it with a profound ecclesial spirit, nourishing their own reflection with prayer and looking to the great riches, not yet fully explored, of the medieval mystic tradi-

tion, especially that represented by luminous models such
as Hildegard of Bingen.

The Rhenish mystic is also the author of other writings, two of which are particularly important since, like
Scivias, they record her mystical visions: they are the *Liber
vitae meritorum* (Book of the merits of life) and the *Liber
divinorum operum* (Book of the divine works), also called
De operatione Dei. In the former she describes a unique
and powerful vision of God who gives life to the cosmos
with his power and his light. Hildegard stresses the deep
relationship that exists between man and God and reminds us that the whole creation, of which man is the
summit, receives life from the Trinity. The work is cen-
tered on the relationship between virtue and vice, which
is why human beings must face the daily challenge of vice
that distances them on their way towards God and of virtue that benefits them. The invitation is to distance themselves from evil in order to glorify God and, after a virtu-
ous existence, enter the life that consists "wholly of joy." In
her second work that many consider her masterpiece she
once again describes creation in its relationship with God
and the centrality of the human being, expressing a strong
Christo-centrism with a biblical-Patristic flavor. The saint,
who presents five visions inspired by the Prologue of the
Gospel according to St. John, cites the words of the Son
to the Father: "The whole task that you wanted and entrusted to me I have carried out successfully, and so here I
am in you and you in me and we are one" (*Pars III, Visio
X: PL* 197, 1025a).

Finally, in other writings Hildegard manifests the versatility of interests and cultural vivacity of the female monasteries of the Middle Ages, in a manner contrary to the prejudices which still weighed on that period. Hildegard took an interest in medicine and in the natural sciences as well as in music, since she was endowed with artistic talent. Thus she composed hymns, antiphons, and songs, gathered under the title: *Symphonia Harmoniae Caelestium Revelationum* (Symphony of the Harmony of Heavenly Revelations), that were performed joyously in her monasteries, spreading an atmosphere of tranquillity, and that have also come down to us. For her, the entire creation is a symphony of the Holy Spirit who is in himself joy and jubilation.

The popularity that surrounded Hildegard impelled many people to seek her advice. It is for this reason that we have so many of her letters at our disposal. Many male and female monastic communities turned to her, as well as Bishops and Abbots. And many of her answers still apply for us. For instance, Hildegard wrote these words to a community of women religious: "The spiritual life must be tended with great dedication. At first the effort is burdensome because it demands the renunciation of caprices of the pleasures of the flesh and of other such things. But if she lets herself be enthralled by holiness a holy soul will find even contempt for the world sweet and lovable. All that is needed is to take care that the soul does not shrivel" (E. Gronau,

The spiritual life must be tended with great dedication.

Hildegard. Vita di una donna profetica alle origini dell'età moderna, Milan 1996, p. 402). And when the Emperor Frederic Barbarossa caused a schism in the Church by supporting at least three anti-popes against Alexander III, the legitimate Pope, Hildegard did not hesitate, inspired by her visions, to remind him that even he, the Emperor, was subject to God's judgment. With fearlessness, a feature of every prophet, she wrote to the Emperor these words as spoken by God: "You will be sorry for this wicked conduct of the godless who despise me! Listen, O King, if you wish to live! Otherwise my sword will pierce you!" (*ibid.,* p. 412).

With the spiritual authority with which she was endowed, in the last years of her life Hildegard set out on journeys, despite her advanced age and the uncomfortable conditions of travel, in order to speak to the people of God. They all listened willingly, even when she spoke severely: they considered her a messenger sent by God. She called above all the monastic communities and the clergy to a life in conformity with their vocation. In a special way Hildegard countered the movement of German *cátari* (Cathars). They (*cátari* means literally "pure") advocated a radical reform of the Church, especially to combat the abuses of the clergy. She harshly reprimanded them for seeking to subvert the very nature of the Church, reminding them that a true renewal of the ecclesial community is obtained with a sincere spirit of repentance and a demanding process of conversion, rather than with a change of structures. This is a message that we should never forget.

Let us always invoke the Holy Spirit, so that he may inspire in the Church holy and courageous women, like St. Hildegard of Bingen, who, developing the gifts they have received from God, make their own special and valuable contribution to the spiritual development of our communities and of the Church in our time.

CHAPTER TWO

St. Clare of Assisi[1]

One of the best-loved saints is without a doubt St. Clare of Assisi who lived in the thirteenth century and was a contemporary of St. Francis. Her testimony shows us how indebted the Church is to courageous women, full of faith like her, who can give a crucial impetus to the Church's renewal.

So who was Clare of Assisi? To answer this question we possess reliable sources: not only the ancient biographies, such as that of Tommaso da Celano, but also the *Proceedings* of the cause of her canonization that the Pope promoted only a few month after Clare's death and that contain the depositions of those who had lived a long time with her.

Born in 1193, Clare belonged to a wealthy, aristocratic family. She renounced her noble status and wealth to live in humility and poverty, adopting the lifestyle that Francis of Assisi recommended. Although her parents were planning a marriage for her with some important figure, as was then the custom, Clare, with a daring act inspired by her deep desire to follow Christ and her admiration for Fran-

---

[1] Pope Benedict XVI, General Audience, September 15, 2010.

cis, at the age of eighteen left her family home and, in the
company of a friend, Bona di Guelfuccio, made her way in
secret to the Friars Minor at the little Church of the Por-
tiuncula. It was the evening of Palm Sunday in 1211. In
the general commotion, a highly symbolic act took place:
while his companions lit torches, Francis cut off Clare's
hair and she put on a rough penitential habit. From that
moment she had become the virgin bride of Christ, humble and poor, and she consecrated herself totally to him.
Like Clare and her companions, down through history in-
numerable women have been fascinated by love for Christ
which, with the beauty of his Divine Person, fills their
hearts. And the entire Church, through the mystical nuptial vocation of consecrated virgins, appears what she will
be forever: the pure and beautiful Bride of Christ.

In one of the four letters that Clare sent to St. Agnes of
Prague the daughter of the King of Bohemia, who wished
to follow in Christ's footsteps, she speaks of Christ, her
beloved Spouse, with nuptial words that may be surprising
but are nevertheless moving: "When you have loved [him]
you shall be chaste; when you have touched [him] you
shall become purer; when you have accepted [him] you
shall be a virgin. Whose power is stronger, whose generosity is more elevated, whose appearance more beautiful,
whose love more tender, whose courtesy more gracious.
In whose embrace you are already caught up; who has
adorned your breast with precious stones ... and placed on
your head a golden crown as a sign [to all] of your holiness" (*First Letter to Blessed Agnes of Prague: FF,* 2862).

Especially at the beginning of her religious experience, Francis of Assisi was not only a teacher to Clare whose teachings she was to follow but also a brotherly friend. The friendship between these two saints is a very beautiful and important aspect. Indeed, when two pure souls on fire with the same love for God meet, they find in their friendship with each other a powerful incentive to advance on the path of perfection. Friendship is one of the noblest and loftiest human sentiments which divine Grace purifies and transfigures. Like St. Francis and St. Clare, other saints too experienced profound friendship on the journey towards Christian perfection. Examples are St. Francis de Sales and St. Jane Frances de Chantal. And St. Francis de Sales himself wrote: "It is a blessed thing to love on earth as we hope to love in heaven, and to begin that friendship here which is to endure for ever there. I am not now speaking of simple charity, a love due to all mankind, but of that spiritual friendship which binds souls together, leading them to share devotions and spiritual interests, so as to have but one mind between them" (*The Introduction to a Devout Life, III*, 19).

After spending a period of several months at other monastic communities, resisting the pressure of her relatives who did not at first approve of her decision, Clare settled with her first companions at the Church of San Damiano where the Friars Minor had organized a small convent for them. She lived in this Monastery for more than forty years, until her death in 1253. A first-hand description has come down to us of how these women lived in those years at the beginning of the Franciscan movement. It is the admiring account of Jacques de Vitry, a Flemish Bishop who came to Italy on a visit. He declared that he had encountered a large number of men and women of every social class who, having "left all things for Christ, fled the world. They called themselves Friars Minor and Sisters Minor [Lesser] and are held in high esteem by the Lord Pope and the Cardinals.... The women live together in various homes not far from the city. They receive nothing but live on the work of their own hands. And they are deeply troubled and pained at being honored more than they would like to be by both clerics and lay people" (*Letter of October* 1216: *FF,* 2205, 2207).

Jacques de Vitry had perceptively noticed a characteristic trait of Franciscan spirituality about which Clare was deeply sensitive: the radicalism of poverty associated with total trust in Divine Providence. For this reason, she acted with great determination, obtaining from Pope Gregory IX or, probably, already from Pope Innocent III, the so-called *Privilegium Paupertatis* (cf. *FF,* 3279). On the basis of this privilege Clare and her companions at San Damiano could not possess any material property. This was a truly extraordinary exception in comparison with the canon law then in force but the ecclesiastical authorities of that time permitted it, appreciating the fruits of evangelical holiness that they recognized in the way of life of Clare and her sisters. This shows that even in the centuries of the Middle Ages the role of women was not secondary but on the contrary considerable. In this regard, it is useful to remember that Clare was the first woman in the Church's history who composed a written Rule, submitted for the Pope's approval, to ensure the preservation of Francis of Assisi's charism in all the communities of women large numbers of which were already springing up in her time that wished to draw inspiration from the example of Francis and Clare.

In the Convent of San Damiano, Clare practiced heroically the virtues that should distinguish every Christian: humility, a spirit of piety, and penitence and charity. Although she was the superior, she wanted to serve the sick sisters herself and joyfully subjected herself to the most menial tasks. In fact, charity overcomes all resistance and whoever loves, joyfully performs every sacrifice. Her faith in

Clare practiced heroically the virtues that should distinguish every Christian: humility, a spirit of piety, and penitence and charity.

the Real Presence of Christ in the Eucharist was so great that twice a miracle happened. Simply by showing to them the Most Blessed Sacrament distanced the Saracen mercenaries, who were on the point of attacking the Convent of San Damiano and pillaging the city of Assisi.

Such episodes, like other miracles whose memories live on, prompted Pope Alexander IV to canonize her in 1255, only two years after her death, outlining her eulogy in the Bull on the Canonization of St. Clare. In it we read: "How powerful was the illumination of this light and how strong the brightness of this source of light. Truly this light was kept hidden in the cloistered life; and, outside the walls, shone with gleaming rays; Clare in fact lay hidden, but her life was revealed to all. Clare was silent, but her fame was shouted out" (*FF,* 3284). And this is exactly how it is, dear friends: those who change the world for the better are holy, they transform it permanently, instilling in it the energies that only love inspired by the Gospel can elicit. The saints are humanity's great benefactors!

St. Clare's spirituality, the synthesis of the holiness she proposed is summed up in the fourth letter she wrote to St. Agnes of Prague. St. Clare used an image very widespread in the Middle Ages that dates back to Patristic times: the mirror. And she invited her friend in Prague to reflect herself in that mirror of the perfection of every virtue which is the Lord himself. She wrote: "Happy, indeed, is the one permitted to share in this sacred banquet so as to be joined with all the feelings of her heart (to Christ) whose beauty all the blessed hosts of the Heavens unceasingly admire, whose affection moves, whose contemplation invigorates, whose generosity fills, whose sweetness replenishes, whose remembrance pleasantly brings light, whose fragrance will revive the dead, and whose glorious vision will bless all the citizens of the heavenly Jerusalem, because the vision of him is the *splendor of everlasting glory, the radiance of everlasting light, and a mirror without tarnish.* Look into this mirror every day, O Queen, spouse of Jesus Christ, and continually examine your face in it, so that in this way you may adorn yourself completely, inwardly and outwardly.... In this mirror shine blessed poverty, holy humility, and charity beyond words..." (*Fourth Letter to Blessed Agnes of Prague, FF,* 2901-2903).

Grateful to God who gives us saints who speak to our hearts and offer us an example of Christian life to imitate, I would like to end with the same words of blessing that St. Clare composed for her Sisters and which the Poor Clares, who play a precious role in the Church with their prayer and with their work, still preserve today with great devotion. These are words in which the full tenderness of her spiritual motherhood emerges: "I give you my blessing now while living, and after my death, in as far as I may: nay, even more than I may, I call down on you all the blessings that the Father of mercies has bestowed and continues to bestow on his spiritual sons and daughters both in Heaven and on earth, and with which a spiritual father and mother have blessed and will bless their spiritual sons and daughters. Amen" (*FF,* 2856).

CHAPTER THREE

St. Matilda of Hackeborn[1]

St. Matilda of Hackeborn, one of the great figures of the convent of Helfta, lived in the thirteenth century. Her sister, St. Gertrude the Great, tells of the special graces that God granted to St. Matilda in the sixth book of *Liber Specialis Gratiae* (Book of Special Grace), which states: "What we have written is very little in comparison with what we have omitted. We are publishing these things solely for the glory of God and the usefulness of our neighbor, for it would seem wrong to us to keep quiet about the many graces that Matilda received from God, not so much for herself, in our opinion, but for us and for those who will come after us" (Mechthild von Hackeborn, *Liber specialis gratiae,* VI, 1).

This work was written by St. Gertrude and by another sister of Helfta and has a unique story. At the age of fifty, Matilda went through a grave spiritual crisis, as well as physical suffering. In this condition she confided to two of her sisters who were friends the special graces with which God had guided her since childhood. However, she did not know that they were writing it all down. When she found out she was deeply upset and distressed. However,

_____
[1] Pope Benedict XVI, General Audience, September 29, 2010.

the Lord reassured her, making her realize that all that had been written was for the glory of God and for the benefit of her neighbor (cf. *ibid.,* II, 25; V, 20). This work, therefore, is the principal source to refer to for information on the life and spirituality of our saint.

With her we are introduced into the family of Baron von Hackeborn, one of the noblest, richest, and most powerful barons of Thuringia, related to the Emperor Frederick II, and we enter the Convent of Helfta in the most glorious period of its history. The Baron had already given one daughter to the convent, Gertrude of Hackeborn (1231/1232 - 1291/1292). She was gifted with an outstanding personality. She was Abbess for forty years, capable of giving the spirituality of the convent a particular hallmark and of bringing it to an extraordinary flourishing as the center of mysticism and culture, a school for scientific and theological training. Gertrude offered the nuns an intellectual training of a high standard that enabled them to cultivate a spirituality founded on Sacred Scripture, on the Liturgy, on the Patristic tradition, on the Cistercian Rule and spirituality, with a particular love for St. Bernard of Clairvaux and William of Saint-Thierry. She was a real teacher, exemplary in all things, in evangelical radicalism and in apostolic zeal. Matilda, from childhood, accepted and enjoyed the spiritual and cultural atmosphere created by her sister, later giving it her own personal hallmark.

Matilda was born in 1241 or 1242 in the Castle of Helfta. She was the Baron's third daughter. When she was seven she went with her mother to visit her sister Gertrude in the Convent of Rodersdorf. She was so enchanted by this environment that she ardently desired to belong to it. She entered as a schoolgirl and in 1258 became a nun at the convent, which in the meantime had moved to Helfta, to the property of the Hackeborns. She was distinguished by her humility, her fervor, her friendliness, the clarity and the innocence of her life, and by the familiarity and intensity with which she lived her relationship with God, the Virgin, and the saints. She was endowed with lofty natural and spiritual qualities such as knowledge, intelligence, familiarity with the humanities, and a marvelously sweet voice: everything suited her to being a true treasure for the convent from every point of view (*ibid., Proem.*). Thus when "God's nightingale," as she was called, was still very young she became the principal of the convent's school, choir mistress, and novice mistress, offices that she fulfilled with talent and unflagging zeal, not only for the benefit of the nuns but for anyone who wanted to draw on her wisdom and goodness.

Illumined by the divine gift of mystic contemplation, Matilda wrote many prayers. She was a teacher of faithful doctrine and deep humility, a counselor, comforter, and guide in discernment. We read: "She distributed doctrine in an abundance never previously seen at the convent, and alas, we are rather afraid that nothing like it will ever be seen again. The sisters would cluster round her to hear the word of God, as if she were a preacher." She was the refuge and consoler of all and, by a unique gift of God, was endowed with the grace of being able to reveal freely the secrets of the heart of each one. Many people, not only in the convent but also outsiders, religious, and lay people, who came from afar, testified that this holy virgin had freed them from their afflictions and that they had never known such comfort as they found near her. *"Furthermore, she composed and taught so many prayers that if they were gathered together they would make a book larger than a Psalter"* (*ibid.*, VI, 1).

In 1261 a five-year-old girl came to the convent. Her name was Gertrude: She was entrusted to the care of Matilda, just twenty years of age, who taught her and guided her in the spiritual life until she not only made her into an excellent disciple but also her confidante. In 1271 or 1272, Matilda of Magdeburg also entered the convent. So it was that this place took in four great women, two Gertrudes and two Matildas, the glory of German monasticism. During her long life which she spent in the convent, Matilda was afflicted with continuous and intense bouts of suffering, to which she added the very harsh penances chosen for the conversion of sinners. In this manner she participated in the Lord's Passion until the end of her life (cf. *ibid.*, VI, 2). Prayer and contemplation were the life-giving *humus* of her existence: her revelations, her teachings, her service to her neighbor, her journey in faith and in love have their root and their context here. In the first book of the work, *Liber Specialis Gratiae,* the nuns wrote down Matilda's

Prayer and contemplation were the life-giving humus of her existence.

confidences pronounced on the Feasts of the Lord, the saints and, especially, of the Blessed Virgin. This saint had a striking capacity for living the various elements of the Liturgy, even the simplest, and bringing it into the daily life of the convent. Some of her images, expressions, and applications are at times distant from our sensibility today, but, if we were to consider monastic life and her task as mistress and choir mistress, we should grasp her rare ability as a teacher and educator who, starting from the Liturgy, helped her sisters to live intensely every moment of monastic life.

Matilda gave an emphasis in liturgical prayer to the canonical hours, to the celebration of Holy Mass and, especially, to Holy Communion. Here she was often rapt in ecstasy in profound intimacy with the Lord in his most ardent and sweetest Heart, carrying on a marvelous conversation in which she asked for inner illumination, while interceding in a special way for her community and her sisters. At the center are the mysteries of Christ which the Virgin Mary constantly recommends to people so that they may walk on the path of holiness: "If you want true holiness, be close to my Son; he is holiness itself that sanctifies all things" (*ibid.*, I, 40). The whole world, the Church, benefactors, and sinners were present in her intimacy with God. For her, heaven and earth were united.

Her visions, her teachings, the events of her life are described in words reminiscent of liturgical and biblical language. In this way it is possible to comprehend her deep knowledge of Sacred Scripture, which was her daily bread.

She had constant recourse to the Scriptures, making the most of the biblical texts read in the Liturgy, and drawing from them symbols, terms, countryside, images, and famous figures. She had a special love for the Gospel: "The words of the Gospel were a marvelous nourishment for her and in her heart stirred feelings of such sweetness that, because of her enthusiasm, she was often unable to finish reading it.... The way in which she read those words was so fervent that it inspired devotion in everyone. Thus when she was singing in the choir, she was completely absorbed in God, uplifted by such ardor that she sometimes expressed her feelings in gestures.... On other occasions, since she was rapt in ecstasy, she did not hear those who were calling or touching her and came back with difficulty to the reality of the things around her" (*ibid.*, VI, 1). In one of her visions, Jesus himself recommended the Gospel to her; opening the wound in his most gentle Heart, he said to her: "consider the immensity of my love: if you want to know it well, nowhere will you find it more clearly expressed than in the Gospel. No one has ever heard expressed stronger or more tender sentiments than these: '*As my father has loved me, so I have loved you*' (Jn 15: 9)" (*ibid.*, I, 22).

Dear friends, personal and liturgical prayer, especially the Liturgy of the Hours and Holy Mass are at the root of St. Matilda of Hackeborn's spiritual experience. In letting herself be guided by Sacred Scripture and nourished by the Bread of the Eucharist, she followed a path of close union with the Lord, ever in full fidelity to the Church. This is also a strong invitation to us to intensify our friendship with the Lord, especially through daily prayer and attentive, faithful, and active participation in Holy Mass. The Liturgy is a great school of spirituality.

Her disciple Gertrude gives a vivid picture of St. Matilda of Hackeborn's last moments. They were very difficult but illumined by the presence of the Blessed Trinity, of the Lord, of the Virgin Mary, and of all the saints, even Gertrude's sister by blood. When the time came in which the Lord chose to gather her to him, she asked him to let her live longer in suffering for the salvation of souls, and Jesus was pleased with this further sign of her love.

Matilda was fifty-eight years old. The last leg of her journey was marked by eight years of serious illness. Her work and the fame of her holiness spread far and wide. When her time came, "the God of majesty ... the one delight of the soul that loves him ... sang to her: *Venite vos, benedicti Patris mei.... Venite, o voi che siete i benedetti dal Padre mio, venite a ricevere il regno ...* and he united her with his glory" (*ibid.*, VI, 8).

May St. Matilda of Hackeborn commend us to the Sacred Heart of Jesus and to the Virgin Mary. She invites us to praise the Son with the Heart of the Mother, and to praise Mary with the Heart of the Son: "I greet you, O most deeply venerated Virgin, in that sweetest of dews which from the Heart of the Blessed Trinity spread within you; I greet you in the glory and joy in which you now rejoice forever, you who were chosen in preference to all the creatures of the earth and of Heaven even before the world's creation! Amen" (*ibid.*, I, 45).

CHAPTER FOUR

St. Gertrude the Great[1]

St. Gertrude the Great, brings us once again to the Monastery of Helfta, where several of the Latin-German masterpieces of religious literature were written by women. Gertrude belonged to this world. She is one of the most famous mystics, the only German woman to be called "Great," because of her cultural and evangelical stature: her life and her thought had a unique impact on Christian spirituality. She was an exceptional woman, endowed with special natural talents and extraordinary gifts of grace, the most profound humility and ardent zeal for her neighbor's salvation. She was in close communion with God both in contemplation and in her readiness to go to the help of those in need.

At Helfta, she measured herself systematically, so to speak, with her teacher, Matilda of Hackeborn (see previous chapter). Gertrude came into contact with Matilda of Magdeburg, another medieval mystic, and grew up under the wing of Abbess Gertrude, motherly, gentle, and demanding. From these three sisters she drew precious experience and wisdom; she worked them into a synthesis of

---

[1] Pope Benedict XVI, General Audience, October 6, 2010.

her own, continuing on her religious journey with bound-less trust in the Lord. Gertrude expressed the riches of her spirituality not only in her monastic world, but also and above all in the biblical, liturgical, Patristic, and Benedic-tine contexts, with a highly personal hallmark and great skill in communicating.

Gertrude was born on January 6, 1256, on the Feast of the Epiphany, but nothing is known of her parents nor of the place of her birth. Gertrude wrote that the Lord him-self revealed to her the meaning of this first uprooting: "I have chosen you for my abode because I am pleased that all that is lovable in you is my work.... For this very reason I have distanced you from all your relatives, so that no one may love you for reasons of kinship and that I may be the sole cause of the affection you receive" (*The Revelations,* I, 16, Siena 1994, pp. 76-77).

When she was five years old, in 1261, she entered the monastery for formation and education, a common prac-tice in that period. Here she spent her whole life, the most important stages of which she herself points out. In her memoirs she recalls that the Lord equipped her in advance with forbearing patience and infinite mercy, forgetting the years of her childhood, adolescence, and youth, which she spent, she wrote, "in such mental blindness that I would have been capable ... of thinking, saying, or doing without remorse everything I liked and wherever I could, had you not armed me in advance, with an inherent horror of evil and a natural inclination for good and with the external vigilance of others, I would have behaved like a pagan ...

in spite of desiring you since childhood, that is since my fifth year of age, when I went to live in the Benedictine shrine of religion to be educated among your most devout friends" (*ibid.*, II, 23, p. 140f.).

Gertrude was an extraordinary student, she learned everything that can be learned of the sciences of the *trivium* and *quadrivium*, the education of that time; she was fascinated by knowledge and threw herself into profane studies with zeal and tenacity, achieving scholastic successes beyond every expectation. If we know nothing of her origins, she herself tells us about her youthful passions: literature, music and song, and the art of miniature painting captivated her. She had a strong, determined, ready, and impulsive temperament. She often says that she was negligent; she recognizes her shortcomings and humbly asks forgiveness for them. She also humbly asks for advice and prayers for her conversion. Some features of her temperament and faults were to accompany her to the end of her life, so as to amaze certain people who wondered why the Lord had favored her with such a special love.

From being a student she moved on to dedicate herself totally to God in monastic life, and for twenty years nothing exceptional occurred: study and prayer were her main activities. Because of her gifts she shone out among the sisters; she was tenacious in consolidating her culture in various fields.

Nevertheless during Advent of 1280 she began to feel disgusted with all this and realized the vanity of it all. On January 27, 1281, a few days before the Feast of the Purification of the Virgin, towards the hour of Compline in the evening, the Lord with his illumination dispelled her deep anxiety. With gentle sweetness he calmed the distress that anguished her, a torment that Gertrude saw even as a gift of God, "to pull down that tower of vanity and curiosity which, although I had both the name and habit of a nun alas I had continued to build with my pride, so that at least in this manner I might find the way for you to show me your salvation" (*ibid.,* II, p. 87). She had a vision of a young man who, in order to guide her through the tangle of thorns that surrounded her soul, took her by the hand. In that hand Gertrude recognized "the precious traces of the wounds that abrogated all the acts of accusation of our enemies" (*ibid.,* II, 1, p. 89), and thus recognized the One who saved us with his Blood on the Cross: Jesus.

From that moment her life of intimate communion with the Lord was intensified, especially in the most important liturgical seasons Advent-Christmas, Lent-Easter, the feasts of Our Lady even when illness prevented her from going to the choir. This was the same liturgical *humus* as that of Matilda, her teacher; but Gertrude describes it with simpler, more linear images, symbols, and terms that are more realistic, and her references to the Bible, to the Fathers, and to the Benedictine world are more direct.

Her biographer points out two directions of what we might describe as her own particular "conversion": *in study,* with the radical passage from profane, humanistic studies to the study of theology, and in *monastic obser-*

vance, with the passage from a life that she describes as *negligent,* to the life of intense, mystical prayer, with exceptional missionary zeal. The Lord who had chosen her from her mother's womb and who since her childhood had made her partake of the banquet of monastic life, called her again with his grace "from external things to inner life and from earthly occupations to love for spiritual things." Gertrude understood that she was remote from him, *in the region of unlikeness,* as she said with Augustine; that she had dedicated herself with excessive greed to liberal studies, to human wisdom, overlooking spiritual knowledge, depriving herself of the taste for true wisdom; she was then led to the mountain of contemplation where she cast off her former self to be re-clothed in the new. "From a grammarian she became a theologian, with the unflagging and attentive reading of all the sacred books that she could lay her hands on or contrive to obtain. She filled her heart with the most useful and sweet sayings of Sacred Scripture. Thus she was always ready with some inspired and edifying word to satisfy those who came to consult her while having at her fingertips the most suitable scriptural texts to refute any erroneous opinion and silence her opponents" (*ibid.,* I, 1, p. 25).

She filled her heart with the most useful and sweet sayings of Sacred Scripture.

Gertrude transformed all this into an apostolate: she devoted herself to writing and popularizing the truth of faith with clarity and simplicity, with grace and persuasion, serving the Church faithfully and lovingly so as to be helpful to and appreciated by theologians and devout people.

Little of her intense activity has come down to us, partly because of the events that led to the destruction of the Monastery of Helfta. In addition to *The Herald of Divine Love* and *The Revelations*, we still have her *Spiritual Exercises,* a rare jewel of mystical spiritual literature.

In religious observance our saint was "a firm pillar… a very powerful champion of justice and truth" (*ibid.,* I, 1, p. 26), her biographer says. By her words and example she kindled great fervor in other people. She added to the prayers and penances of the monastic rule others with such devotion and such trusting abandonment in God that she inspired in those who met her an awareness of being in the Lord's presence. In fact, God made her understand that he had called her to be an instrument of his grace. Gertrude herself felt unworthy of this immense divine treasure, and confesses that she had not safeguarded it or made enough of it. She exclaimed: "Alas! If you had given me to remember you, unworthy as I am, by even only a straw, I would have viewed it with greater respect and reverence than I have had for all your gifts!" (*ibid.,* II, 5, p. 100). Yet, in recognizing her poverty and worthlessness she adhered to God's will, "because," she said, "I have so little profited from your graces that I cannot resolve to believe that they were lavished upon me solely for my own use, since no one can thwart your eternal wisdom. Therefore, O Giver of every good thing who has freely lavished upon me gifts so undeserved, in order that, in reading this, the heart of at least one of your friends may be moved at the thought that zeal for souls has induced you to leave such a priceless gem for so long in the abominable mud of my heart" (*ibid.,* II, 5, p. 100f.).

Two favors in particular were dearer to her than any other, as Gertrude herself writes: "The stigmata of your salvation-bearing wounds which you impressed upon me, as it were, like a valuable necklace, in my heart, and the profound and salutary wound of love with which you marked it.

"You flooded me with your gifts, of such beatitude that even were I to live for 1,000 years with no consolation neither interior nor exterior the memory of them would suffice to comfort me, to enlighten me, to fill me with gratitude. Further, you wished to introduce me into the inestimable intimacy of your friendship by opening to me in various ways that most noble sacrarium of your Divine Being which is your Divine Heart.... To this accumulation of benefits you added that of giving me as Advocate the Most Holy Virgin Mary, your Mother, and often recommended me to her affection, just as the most faithful of bridegrooms would recommend his beloved bride to his own mother" (*ibid.,* II, 23, p. 145).

Looking forward to never-ending communion, she ended her earthly life on November 17, 1301 or 1302, at the age of about forty-six. In the seventh Exercise, that of preparation for death, St. Gertrude wrote: "O Jesus, you who are immensely dear to me, be with me always, so that my heart may stay with you and that your love may endure with me with no possibility of division; and bless my passing, so that my spirit, freed from the bonds of the flesh, may immediately find rest in you. Amen" (*Spiritual Exercises,* Milan 2006, p. 148).

It seems obvious to me that these are not only things of the past, of history; rather St. Gertrude's life lives on as a lesson of Christian life, of an upright path, and shows us that the heart of a happy life, of a true life, is friendship with the Lord Jesus. And this friendship is learned in love for Sacred Scripture, in love for the Liturgy, in profound faith, in love for Mary, so as to be ever more truly acquainted with God himself and hence with true happiness, which is the goal of our life. Many thanks.

CHAPTER FIVE

Bl. Angela of Foligno[1]

Bl. Angela of Foligno was a great medieval mystic who lived in the thirteenth century. People are usually fascinated by the consummate experience of union with God that she reached, but perhaps they give too little consideration to her first steps, her conversion, and the long journey that led from her starting point, the "great fear of hell," to her goal, total union with the Trinity. The first part of Angela's life was certainly not that of a fervent disciple of the Lord. She was born into a well-off family in about 1248. Her father died, and she was brought up in a somewhat superficial manner by her mother. She was introduced at a rather young age into the worldly circles of the town of Foligno, where she met a man whom she married at the age of twenty and to whom she bore children. Her life was so carefree that she was even contemptuous of the so-called "penitents," who abounded in that period; they were people who, in order to follow Christ, sold their possessions and lived in prayer, fasting, in service to the Church, and in charity.

---

[1] Pope Benedict XVI, General Audience, October 13, 2010.

Certain events, such as the violent earthquake in 1279, a hurricane, the endless war against Perugia and its harsh consequences, affected the life of Angela who little by little became aware of her sins, until she took a decisive step. In 1285 she called upon St. Francis, who appeared to her in a vision and asked his advice on making a good general Confession. She then went to Confession with a Friar in San Feliciano. Three years later, on her path of conversion she reached another turning point: she was released from any emotional ties. In the space of a few months, her mother's death was followed by the death of her husband and those of all her children. She therefore sold her possessions and in 1291 enrolled in the Third Order of St. Francis. She died in Foligno on January 4, 1309.

The Book of Visions and Instructions of Bl. Angela of Foligno, in which is gathered the documentation on our Blessed, tells the story of this conversion and points out the necessary means: penance, humility, and tribulation; and it recounts the steps, Angela's successive experiences which began in 1285. Remembering them after she had experienced them, Angela then endeavored to recount them through her friar confessor, who faithfully transcribed them, seeking later to sort them into stages which he called "steps or mutations" but without managing to put them entirely in order (cf. *Il Libro della beata Angela da Foligno,* Cinisello Balsamo 1990, p. 51). This was because for Bl. Angela the experience of union meant the total involvement of both the spiritual and physical senses, and she was left with only a "shadow" in her mind, as it were, of what she had "understood" during her ecstasies. "I truly heard these words," she confessed after a mystical ecstasy, but it is in no way possible for me to know or tell of what I saw and understood, or of what he [God] showed me, although I would willingly reveal what I understood with the words that I heard, but it was an absolutely ineffable abyss." Angela of Foligno presented her mystical "life," without elaborating on it herself because these were divine illuminations that were communicated suddenly and unexpectedly to her soul. Her friar confessor too had difficulty in reporting these events, "partly because of her great and wonderful reserve concerning the divine gifts" (*ibid.*, p. 194). In addition to Angela's difficulty in expressing her mystical experience was the difficulty her listeners found in understanding her. It was a situation which showed clearly that the one true Teacher, Jesus, dwells in the heart of every believer and wants to take total possession of it. So it was with Angela, who wrote to a spiritual son: "My son, if you were to see my heart you would be absolutely obliged to do everything God wants, because my heart is God's heart and God's heart is mine." Here St. Paul's words ring out: "It is no longer I who live, but Christ who lives in me" (Gal 2: 20).

Let us then consider only a few "steps" of our Blessed's rich spiritual journey. The first, in fact, is an introduction: "It was the knowledge of sin," as she explained, "after which my soul was deeply afraid of damnation; in this stage I shed bitter tears" (*Il Libro della beata Angela da Foligno,* p. 39). This "dread" of hell corresponds to the type of faith that Angela had at the time of her "conversion"; it was a faith still poor in charity, that is, in love of God. Repentance, the fear of hell, and penance unfolded to Angela the prospect of the sorrowful "Way of the Cross," which from the eighth to the fifteenth stages was to lead her to the "way of love." Her friar confessor recounted: "The faithful woman then told me: 'I have had this divine revelation: after the things you have written, write that anyone who wishes to preserve grace must not lift the eyes of his soul from the Cross, either in the joy or in the sadness that I grant or permit him'" (*ibid.*, p. 143). However, in this phase Angela "did not yet feel love." She said: "The soul feels shame and bitterness and does not yet feel love but suffering" (*ibid.*, p. 39), and is unrequited.

Angela felt she should give something to God in reparation for her sins, but slowly came to realize that she had nothing to give him, indeed, that she "was nothing" before him. She understood that it would not be her will to give her God's love, for her will could give only her own "nothingness," her "non-love." As she was to say: only "true and pure love, that comes from God, is in the soul and ensures that one recognizes one's own shortcomings and the divine goodness.... Such love brings the soul to Christ, and it understands with certainty that in him no deception can be found or can exist. No particle of worldly love can be mingled with this love" (*ibid.*, p. 124-125). This meant opening herself solely and totally to God's love whose greatest expression is in Christ: "O my God," she prayed, "make me worthy of knowing the loftiest mystery that your most ardent and ineffable love brought about for our sake, together with the love of the Trinity, in other words the loftiest mystery of your most holy Incarnation.... O incomprehensible love! There is no greater love than this love that brought my God to become man in order to make me God" (*ibid.,* p. 295). However, Angela's heart always bore the wounds of sin; even after a good Confession she would find herself forgiven and yet still stricken by sin, free and yet conditioned by the past, absolved but in need of penance. And the thought of hell accompanied her too, for the greater the progress the soul makes on the way of Christian perfection, the more convinced it is not only of being "unworthy" but also deserving of hell.

And so it was that on this mystical journey Angela understood the central reality in a profound way: what would save her from her "unworthiness" and from "deserving hell" would not be her "union with God" or her possession of the "truth" but Jesus Crucified, "his crucifixion for me," his love.

In the eighth step, she said, "However, I did not yet understand whether my liberation from sins and from hell and conversion to penance was far greater, or his crucifixion for me" (*ibid.,* n. 41). This was the precarious balance between love and suffering, that she felt throughout her arduous journey towards perfection. For this very reason she preferred to contemplate Christ Crucified, because in this vision she saw the perfect balance brought about. On the Cross was the man-God, in a supreme act of suffering which was a supreme act of love. In the third *Instruction* the Blessed insisted on this contemplation and declared: "The more perfectly and purely we see, the more perfectly and purely we love.... Therefore the more we see the God and man, Jesus Christ, the more we are transformed in him through love.... What I said of love ... I also say of suffering: the more the soul contemplates the ineffable suffering of the God and man Jesus Christ the more sorrowful it becomes and is transformed through suffering" (*ibid.,* p. 190-191). Thus, unifying herself with and transforming herself into the love and suffering of Christ Crucified, she was identifying herself with him. Angela's conversion, which began from that Confession in 1285, was to reach maturity only when God's forgiveness appeared to her soul as the freely given gift of the love of the Father, the source of love: "No one can make excuses," she said, "because anyone can love God and he does not ask the soul for more than to love him, because he loves the soul and it is his love" (*ibid.,* p. 76).

> *The more perfectly and purely we see, the more perfectly and purely we love.*

On Angela's spiritual journey the transition from conversion to mystical experience, from what can be expressed to the inexpressible, took place through the Crucified One. He is the "God-man of the Passion," who became her "teacher of perfection." The whole of her mystical experience, therefore, consisted in striving for a perfect "likeness" with him, through ever deeper and ever more radical purifications and transformations. Angela

threw her whole self, body and soul, into this stupen-
dous undertaking, never sparing herself of penance and
suffering, from beginning to end, desiring to die with all
the sorrows suffered by the God-man crucified in order
to be totally transformed in him. "O children of God,"
she recommended, "transform yourselves totally in the
man-God who so loved you that he chose to die for you
a most ignominious and all together unutterably painful
death, and in the most painful and bitterest way. And this
was solely for love of you, O man!" (*ibid.*, p. 247). This
identification also meant experiencing what Jesus himself
experienced: poverty, contempt, and sorrow, because, as
she declared, "through temporal poverty the soul will find
eternal riches; through contempt and shame it will obtain supreme honor and very great glory; through a little
penance, made with pain and sorrow, it will possess with
infinite sweetness and consolation the Supreme Good,
Eternal God" (*ibid.*, p. 293).

From conversion to mystic union with Christ Crucified, to the inexpressible. A very lofty journey, whose secret is constant prayer. "The more you pray," she said, "the
more illumined you will be and the more profoundly and
intensely you will see the supreme Good, the supremely
good Being; the more profoundly and intensely you see
him, the more you will love him; the more you love him
the more he will delight you; and the more he delights
you, the better you will understand him and you will become capable of understanding him. You will then reach

the fullness of light, for you will understand that you cannot understand" (*ibid.,* p. 184).

Dear brothers and sisters, Bl. Angela's life began with a
worldly existence, rather remote from God. Yet her meeting with the figure of St. Francis and, finally, her meeting
with Christ Crucified reawakened her soul to the presence
of God, for the reason that with God alone life becomes
true life, because, in sorrow for sin, it becomes love and
joy. And this is how Bl. Angela speaks to us. Today we all
risk living as though God did not exist; he seems so distant from daily life. However, God has thousands of ways
of his own for each one, to make himself present in the
soul, to show that he exists and knows and loves us. And
Bl. Angela wishes to make us attentive to these signs with
which the Lord touches our soul, attentive to God's presence, so as to learn the way with God and towards God, in
communion with Christ Crucified. Let us pray the Lord
that he make us attentive to the signs of his presence and
that he teach us truly to live.

CHAPTER SIX

St. Elizabeth of Hungary[1]

One of the women of the Middle Ages who inspired the greatest admiration was St. Elizabeth of Hungary, also called St. Elizabeth of Thuringia.

Elizabeth was born in 1207; historians dispute her birthplace. Her father was Andrew II, the rich and powerful King of Hungary. To reinforce political ties he had married the German Countess Gertrude of Andechs-Meran, sister of St. Hedwig who was wife to the Duke of Silesia. Elizabeth, together with her sister and three brothers, spent only the first four years of her childhood at the Hungarian court. She liked playing, music, and dancing; she recited her prayers faithfully and already showed special attention to the poor, whom she helped with a kind word or an affectionate gesture.

Her happy childhood was suddenly interrupted when some knights arrived from distant Thuringia to escort her to her new residence in Central Germany. In fact, complying with the customs of that time, Elizabeth's father had arranged for her to become a Princess of Thuringia. The Landgrave or Count of this region was one of the richest

---

[1] Pope Benedict XVI, General Audience, October 20, 2010.

and most influential sovereigns in Europe at the beginning of the thirteenth century, and his castle was a center of magnificence and culture.

However, the festivities and apparent glory concealed the ambition of feudal princes who were frequently warring with each other and in conflict with the royal and imperial authorities.

In this context the Landgrave Hermann very willingly accepted the betrothal of his son Ludwig to the Hungarian Princess. Elizabeth left her homeland with a rich dowry and a large entourage, including her personal ladies-in-waiting, two of whom were to remain faithful friends to the very end. It is they who left us the precious information on the childhood and life of the saint.

They reached Eisenach after a long journey and made the ascent to the Fortress of Wartburg, the strong castle towering over the city. It was here that the betrothal of Ludwig and Elizabeth was celebrated. In the ensuing years, while Ludwig learned the knightly profession, Elizabeth and her companions studied German, French, Latin, music, literature, and embroidery. Despite the fact that political reasons had determined their betrothal, a sincere love developed between the two young people, enlivened by faith and by the desire to do God's will. On his father's death when Ludwig was eighteen years old, he began to reign over Thuringia.

Elizabeth, however, became the object of critical whispers because her behavior was incongruous with court life. Hence their marriage celebrations were far from sumptuous and a part of the funds destined for the banquet was donated to the poor.

With her profound sensitivity, Elizabeth saw the contradictions between the faith professed and Christian practice. She could not bear compromise. Once, on entering a church on the Feast of the Assumption, she took off her crown, laid it before the Crucifix and, covering her face, lay prostrate on the ground. When her mother-in-law reprimanded her for this gesture, Elizabeth answered: "How can I, a wretched creature, continue to wear a crown of earthly dignity, when I see my King Jesus Christ crowned with thorns?"

She behaved to her subjects in the same way that she behaved to God. Among the *Sayings of the four maids* we find this testimony: "She did not eat any food before ascertaining that it came from her husband's property or legitimate possessions. While she abstained from goods procured illegally, she also did her utmost to provide compensation to those who had suffered violence" (nn. 25 and 37).

She is a true example for all who have roles of leadership: the exercise of authority, at every level, must be lived as a service to justice and charity, in the constant search for the common good.

Elizabeth diligently practiced works of mercy: she would give food and drink to those who knocked at her door; she procured clothing, paid debts, cared for the sick, and buried the dead. Coming down from her castle, she often visited the homes of the poor with her ladies-in-waiting, bringing them bread, meat, flour, and other food. She distributed the food personally and attentively checked the clothing and mattresses of the poor.

This behavior was reported to her husband, who not only was not displeased but answered her accusers, "So long as she does not sell the castle, I am happy with her!"

The miracle of the loaves that were changed into roses fits into this context: while Elizabeth was on her way with her apron filled with bread for the poor, she met her husband who asked her what she was carrying. She opened her apron to show him and, instead of bread, it was full of magnificent roses. This symbol of charity often features in depictions of St. Elizabeth.

Elizabeth's marriage was profoundly happy: she helped her husband to raise his human qualities to a supernatural level and he, in exchange, stood up for his wife's generosity to the poor and for her religious practices. Increasingly admired for his wife's great faith, Ludwig said to her, referring to her attention to the poor, "Dear Elizabeth, it is Christ whom you have cleansed, nourished, and cared for" — a clear witness to how faith and love of God and neighbor strengthen family life and deepen ever more the matrimonial union.

The young couple found spiritual support in the Friars Minor who began to spread through Thuringia in 1222. Elizabeth chose from among them Friar Rodeger (Rüdiger) as her spiritual director. When he told her about the event of the conversion of Francis of Assisi, a rich young merchant, Elizabeth was even more enthusiastic in the journey of her Christian life.

From that time she became even more determined to follow the poor and Crucified Christ, present in poor people. Even when her first son was born, followed by two other children, our saint never neglected her charitable works. She also helped the Friars Minor to build a convent at Halberstadt, of which Friar Rodeger became superior. For this reason Elizabeth's spiritual direction was taken on by Conrad of Marburg.

The farewell to her husband was a hard trial, when, at the end of June in 1227 when Ludwig IV joined the Crusade of the Emperor Frederick II. He reminded his wife that this was traditional for the sovereigns of Thuringia. Elizabeth answered him: "Far be it from me to detain you. I have given my whole self to God and now I must also give you."

However, fever decimated the troops and Ludwig himself fell ill and died in Otranto, before embarking, in September 1227. He was twenty-seven years old. When Elizabeth learned the news, she was so sorrowful that she withdrew in solitude; but then, strengthened by prayer and comforted by the hope of seeing him again in heaven, she began to attend to the affairs of the kingdom.

However, another trial was lying in wait for Elizabeth. Her brother-in-law usurped the government of Thuringia, declaring himself to be the true heir of Ludwig and accusing Elizabeth of being a pious woman incapable of ruling. The young widow, with three children, was banished from the Castle of Wartburg and went in search of a place of refuge. Only two of her ladies remained close to her. They accompanied her and entrusted the three children to the care of Ludwig's friends. Wandering through the villages, Elizabeth worked wherever she was welcomed, looked after the sick, spun thread, and cooked.

During this calvary which she bore with great faith, with patience, and with dedication to God, a few relatives who had stayed faithful to her and viewed her brother-in-law's rule as illegal, restored her reputation. So it was that at the beginning of 1228, Elizabeth received sufficient income to withdraw to the family's castle in Marburg, where her spiritual director, Fra Conrad, also lived.

It was he who reported the following event to Pope Gregory IX: "On Good Friday in 1228, having placed her hands on the altar in the chapel of her city, Eisenach, to which she had welcomed the Friars Minor, in the presence of several friars and relatives Elizabeth renounced her own will and all the vanities of the world. She also wanted to resign all her possessions, but I dissuaded her out of love for the poor. Shortly afterwards she built a hospital, gathered the sick and invalids, and served at her own table the most wretched and deprived. When I reprimanded her for these things, Elizabeth answered that she received from the poor special grace and humility" (*Epistula magistri Conradi*, 14-17).

Elizabeth renounced her own will and all the vanities of the world.

We can discern in this affirmation a certain mystical experience similar to that of St. Francis: the *Poverello* of Assisi declared in his testament, in fact, that serving lepers, which he at first found repugnant, was transformed into sweetness of the soul and of the body (*Testamentum,* 1-3).

Elizabeth spent her last three years in the hospital she founded, serving the sick and keeping watch over the dying. She always tried to carry out the most humble services and repugnant tasks. She became what we might call a consecrated woman in the world (*soror in saeculo*) and, with other friends clothed in grey habits, formed a religious community. It is not by chance that she is the Patroness of the Third Order Regular of St. Francis and of the Franciscan Secular Order.

In November 1231 she was stricken with a high fever. When the news of her illness spread, may people flocked to see her. After about ten days, she asked for the doors to be closed so that she might be alone with God. In the night of November 17, she fell asleep gently in the Lord. The testimonies of her holiness were so many and such that after only four years Pope Gregory IX canonized her and, that same year, the beautiful church built in her honor at Marburg was consecrated.

Dear brothers and sisters, in St. Elizabeth we see how faith and friendship with Christ create a sense of justice, of the equality of all, of the rights of others, and how they create love, charity. And from this charity is born hope too, the certainty that we are loved by Christ and that the love of Christ awaits us, thereby rendering us capable of imitating Christ and of seeing Christ in others.

St. Elizabeth invites us to rediscover Christ, to love him and to have faith; and thereby to find true justice and love, as well as the joy that one day we shall be immersed in divine love, in the joy of eternity with God.

CHAPTER SEVEN

St. Bridget of Sweden[1]

On the eve of the Great Jubilee in anticipation of the Year 2000, Bl. John Paul II proclaimed St. Bridget of Sweden Co-Patroness of the whole of Europe. I would like to present her, her message and the reasons why — still today — this holy woman has much to teach the Church and the world.

We are well acquainted with the events of St. Bridget's life because her spiritual fathers compiled her biography in order to further the process of her canonization immediately after her death in 1373. Bridget was born seventy years earlier, in 1303, in Finster, Sweden, a Northern European nation that for three centuries had welcomed the Christian faith with the same enthusiasm as that with which the saint had received it from her parents, very devout people who belonged to noble families closely related to the reigning house.

We can distinguish *two periods* in this saint's life.

The *first* was characterized by her happily married state. Her husband was called Ulf and he was Governor of an important district of the Kingdom of Sweden.

---

[1] Pope Benedict XVI, General Audience, October 27, 2010.

The marriage lasted for twenty-eight years, until Ulf's death. Eight children were born, the second of whom, Karin (Catherine), is venerated as a saint. This is an eloquent sign of Bridget's dedication to her children's education. Moreover, King Magnus of Sweden so appreciated her pedagogical wisdom that he summoned her to Court for a time, so that she could introduce his young wife, Blanche of Namur, to Swedish culture. Bridget, who was given spiritual guidance by a learned religious who initiated her into the study of the Scriptures, exercised a very positive influence on her family which, thanks to her presence, became a true "domestic church." Together with her husband she adopted the Rule of the Franciscan Tertiaries. She generously practiced works of charity for the poor; she also founded a hospital.

At his wife's side Ulf's character improved and he advanced in the Christian life. On their return from a long pilgrimage to Santiago de Compostela, which they made in 1341 with other members of the family, the couple developed a project of living in continence; but a little while later, in the tranquility of a monastery to which he had retired, Ulf's earthly life ended. This first period of Bridget's life helps us to appreciate what today we could describe as an authentic "conjugal spirituality": together, Christian spouses can make a journey of holiness sustained by the grace of the Sacrament of Marriage. It is often the woman, as happened in the life of St. Bridget and Ulf, who with her religious sensitivity, delicacy and gentleness succeeds in persuading her husband to follow a path of faith. I am thinking with gratitude of the many women who, day after day, illuminate their families with their witness of Christian life, in our time too. May the Lord's Spirit still inspire holiness in Christian spouses today, to show the world the beauty of marriage lived in accordance with the Gospel values: love, tenderness, reciprocal help, fruitfulness in begetting and in raising children, openness and solidarity to the world and participation in the life of the Church.

The *second* period of Bridget's life began when she was widowed. She did not consider another marriage in order to deepen her union with the Lord through prayer, penance and charitable works. Therefore Christian widows too may find in this saint a model to follow. In fact, upon the death of her husband, after distributing her possessions to the poor — although she never became a consecrated religious — Bridget settled near the Cistercian Monastery of Alvastra. Here began the divine revelations that were to accompany her for the rest of her life. Bridget dictated them to her confessors-secretaries, who translated them from Swedish into Latin and gathered them in eight volumes entitled *Revelationes* (Revelations). A supplement followed these books called, precisely, *Revelationes extravagantes* (Supplementary revelations).

St. Bridget's *Revelations* have a very varied content and style. At times the revelations are presented in the form of dialogues between the divine Persons, the Virgin, the saints and even demons; they are dialogues in which Bridget also takes part. At other times, instead, a specific vision is described; and in yet others what the Virgin Mary reveals to her concerning the life and mysteries of the Son. The value of St. Bridget's *Revelations*, sometimes the object of criticism, Bl. John Paul II explained in his Letter *Spes Aedificandi*: "The Church, which recognized Bridget's holiness without ever pronouncing on her individual revelations, has accepted the overall authenticity of her interior experience" (n. 5). Indeed, reading these *Revelations* challenges us on many important topics. For example, the description of Christ's Passion, with very realistic details, frequently recurs. Bridget always had a special devotion to Christ's Passion, contemplating in it God's infinite love for human beings. She boldly places these words on the lips of the Lord who speaks to her: "O my friends, I love my sheep so tenderly that were it possible I would die many other times for each one of them that same death I suffered for the redemption of all" (*Revelationes*, Book I, c. 59). The sorrowful motherhood of Mary, which made her Mediatrix and Mother of Mercy, is also a subject that recurs frequently in the *Revelations*.

In receiving these charisms, Bridget was aware that she had been given a gift of special love on the Lord's part: "My Daughter" — we read in the First Book of *Revelations* — "I have chosen you for myself, love me with all your heart ... more than all that exists in the world" (c. 1). Bridget, moreover, knew well and was firmly convinced that every charism is destined to build up the Church. For this very reason many of her revelations were addressed in the form of admonishments, even severe ones, to the believers of her time, including the religious and political authorities, that they might live a consistent Christian life; but she always reprimanded them with an attitude of respect and of full fidelity to the Magisterium of the Church and in particular to the Successor of the Apostle Peter.

In 1349 Bridget left Sweden for good and went on pilgrimage to Rome. She was not only intending to take part in the Jubilee of the Year 1350 but also wished to obtain from the Pope approval for the Rule of a Religious Order that she was intending to found, called after the Holy Savior and made up of monks and nuns under the authority of the Abbess. This is an element we should not find surprising: in the Middle Ages monastic foundations existed with both male and female branches, but with the practice of the same monastic Rule that provided for the Abbess' direction. In fact, in the great Christian tradition the woman is accorded special dignity and — always based on the example of Mary, Queen of Apostles — a place of her own in the Church, which, without coinciding with the ordained priesthood is equally important for the spiritual growth of the Community.

Furthermore, the collaboration of consecrated men and women, always with respect for their specific vocation, is of great importance in the contem-

Bridget dedicated herself to a life of intense apostolate and prayer.

porary world. In Rome, in the company of her daughter Karin, Bridget dedicated herself to a life of intense apostolate and prayer. And from Rome she went on pilgrimage to various Italian Shrines, in particular to Assisi, the homeland of St. Francis for whom Bridget had always had great devotion. Finally, in 1371, her deepest desire was crowned: to travel to the Holy Land, to which she went accompanied by her spiritual children, a group that Bridget called "the friends of God." In those years the Pontiffs lived at Avignon, a long way from Rome: Bridget addressed a heartfelt plea to them to return to the See of Peter, in the Eternal City. She died in 1373, before Pope Gregory XI returned to Rome definitively. She was buried temporarily in the Church of San Lorenzo in Panisperna in Rome but in 1374 her children, Birger and Karin, took her body back to her homeland, to the Monastery of Vadstena, the headquarters of the Religious Order St. Bridget had founded. The order immediately experienced a considerable expansion.

In 1391 Pope Boniface IX solemnly canonized her. Bridget's holiness, characterized by the multiplicity of her gifts and the experiences that I have wished to recall in this brief biographical and spiritual outline, makes her an eminent figure in European history. In coming from Scandinavia, St. Bridget bears witness to the way Christianity had deeply permeated the life of all the peoples of this Continent. In declaring her Co-Patroness of Europe, Bl. Pope John Paul II hoped that St. Bridget — who lived in the fourteenth century when Western Christianity had not yet been wounded by division — may intercede effectively with God to obtain the grace of full Christian unity so deeply longed for. Let us pray, dear brothers and sisters, for this same intention, which we have very much at heart, and that Europe may always be nourished by its Christian roots, invoking the powerful intercession of St. Bridget of Sweden, a faithful disciple of God and Co-Patroness of Europe.

CHAPTER EIGHT

Marguerite d'Oingt[1]

With Marguerite d'Oingt, we are introduced to Carthusian spirituality which draws its inspiration from the evangelical synthesis lived and proposed by St. Bruno. We do not know the date of her birth, although some place it around 1240. Marguerite came from a powerful family of the old nobility of Lyons, the Oingt. We know that her mother was also called Marguerite, that she had two brothers — Giscard and Louis — and three sisters: Catherine, Elizabeth and Agnes. The latter followed her to the Carthusian monastery, succeeding her as Prioress.

We have no information on her childhood, but from her writings it seems that she spent it peacefully in an affectionate family environment. In fact, to express God's boundless love, she valued images linked to the family, with particular reference to the figure of the father and of the mother. In one of her meditations she prays thus: "Most gentle Lord, when I think of the special graces that you have given me through your solicitude: first of all, how you took care of me since my childhood and how you removed me from the danger of this world and called me

---

[1] Pope Benedict XVI, General Audience, November 3, 2010.

to dedicate myself to your holy service, and how you provided everything that was necessary for me: food, drink, dress and footwear (and you did so) in such a way that I had no occasion to think of these things but of your great mercy" (Marguerite d'Oingt, *Scritti Spirituali*, *Meditazione* V, 100, Cinisello Balsamo, 1997, p. 74).

Again from her meditations we know that she entered the Carthusian monastery of Poleteins in response to the Lord's call, leaving everything behind and accepting the strict Carthusian Rule in order to belong totally to the Lord, to be with him always. She wrote: "Gentle Lord, I left my father and my mother and my siblings and all the things of this world for love of you; but this is very little, because the riches of this world are but thorns that prick; and the more one possesses the more unfortunate one is. And because of this it seems to me that I left nothing other than misery and poverty; but you know, gentle Lord, that if I possessed a gentle thousand worlds and could dispose of them as I pleased, I would abandon everything for love of you; and even if you gave me everything that you possess in heaven and on earth, I would not consider myself satiated until I had you, because you are the life of my soul, I do not have and do not want to have a father and mother outside of you" (*ibid.*, *Meditazione* II, 32, p. 59).

We also have little data on her life in the Carthusian monastery. We know that in 1288 she became its fourth Prioress, a post she held until her death, February 11, 1310. From her writings, however, we do not deduce particular stages in her spiritual itinerary. She conceived the entirety of life as a journey of purification up to full configuration with Christ. He is the book that is written, which is inscribed daily in her own heart and life, in particular his saving Passion. In the work "Speculum," referring to herself in the third person Marguerite stresses that by the Lord's grace "she had engraved in her heart the holy life that Jesus Christ God led on earth, his good example and his good doctrine. She had placed the gentle Jesus Christ so well in her heart that it even seemed to her that he was present and that he had a closed book in his hand, to instruct her" (*ibid.*, I, 2-3, p. 81). "In this book she found written the life that Jesus Christ led on earth, from his birth to his ascension into Heaven" (*ibid.*, I, 12, p. 83). Every day, beginning in the morning, Marguerite dedicated herself to the study of this book. And, when she had looked at it well, she began to read the book of her own conscience, which showed the falsehoods and lies of her own life (cf. *ibid.*, I, 6-7, p. 82); she wrote about herself to help others and to fix more deeply in her heart the grace of the presence of God, so as to make every day of her life marked by comparison with the words and actions of Jesus, with the Book of his life. And she did this so that Christ's life would be imprinted in her soul in a permanent and profound way, until she was able to see the Book internally, that is, until contemplating the mystery of God Trinity (cf. *ibid.*, II, 14-22; III, 23-40, pp. 84-90).

Through her writings, Marguerite gives us some traces of her spirituality, enabling us to understand some features of her personality and of her gifts of governance. She was a very learned woman; she usually wrote in Latin, the language of the erudite, but she also wrote in Provençal, and this too is a rarity: thus her writings are the first of those known to be written in that language. She lived a life rich in mystical experiences described with simplicity, allowing one to intuit the ineffable mystery of God, stressing the limits of the mind to apprehend it and the inadequacy of human language to express it. Marguerite had a linear personality, simple, open, of gentle affectivity, great balance and acute discernment, able to enter into the depths of the human spirit, discerning its limits, its ambiguities, but also its aspirations, the soul's *élan* toward God. She showed an outstanding aptitude for governance, combining her profound mystical spiritual life with service to her sisters and to the community. Significant in this connection is a passage of a letter to her father. She wrote: "My dear father, I wish to inform you that I am very busy because of the needs of our house, so that I am unable to apply my mind to good thoughts; in fact, I have so much to do that I do not know which way to turn. We did not harvest the wheat in the seventh month of the year and our vineyards were destroyed by the storm. Moreover, our church is in such a sorry state that we are obliged to reconstruct it in part" (*ibid., Lettere*, III, 14, p. 127).

A Carthusian nun thus describes the figure of Marguerite: "Revealed through her work is a fascinating personality, of lively intelligence, oriented to speculation and at the same time favored by mystical graces: in a word, a holy and wise woman who is able to express with a certain humor an affectivity altogether spiritual" (*Una Monaca Certosina*; *Certosine*, in the *Dizionario degli Istituti di Perfezione*, Rome, 1975, col. 777). In the dynamism of mystical life, Marguerite valued the experience of natural affections, purified by grace, as a privileged means to understand more profoundly and to endorse divine action with greater alacrity and ardor. The reason lies in the fact that the human person is created in the image of God and is therefore called to build with God a wonderful history of love, allowing himself to be totally involved in his initiative.

The God-Trinity, the God-love who reveals himself in Christ fascinated her, and Marguerite lived a relationship of profound love for the Lord and, in contrast, sees human ingratitude to the point of betrayal, even to the paradox of the Cross. She says that the Cross of Christ is similar to the bench of travail. Jesus' pain is compared with that of a mother. She wrote: "The mother who carried me in her womb suffered greatly in giving birth to me, for a day or a night, but you, most gentle Lord, were tormented for me not only for one night or one day, but for more than 30 years!... How bitterly you suffered because of me throughout your life! And when the moment of delivery arrived, your work was so painful that your holy sweat became as drops of blood which ran down your whole body to the ground" (*ibid.*, *Meditazione* I, 33, p. 59). In evoking the accounts of Jesus' Passion, Margue-

In evoking the accounts of Jesus' Passion, Marguerite contemplated these sorrows with profound compassion.

rite contemplated these sorrows with profound compassion. She said: "You were placed on the hard bed of the Cross, so that you could not move or turn or shake your limbs as a man usually does when suffering great pain, because you were completely stretched and pierced with the nails ... and ... all your muscles and veins were lacerated.... But all these pains... were still not sufficient for you, so much so that you desired that your side be pierced so cruelly by the lance that your defenseless body should be totally ploughed and torn and your precious blood spurted with such violence that it formed a long path, almost as if it were a current." Referring to Mary, she said: "It was no wonder that the sword that lacerated your body also penetrated the heart of your glorious Mother who so wanted to support you ... because your love was loftier than any other love" (*ibid.*, *Meditazione* II, 36-39.42, p. 60f.).

Dear friends, Marguerite d'Oingt invites us to meditate daily on the life of sorrow and love of Jesus and that of his mother, Mary. Here is our hope, the meaning of our existence. From contemplation of Christ's love for us are born the strength and joy to respond with the same love, placing our life at the service of God and of others. With Marguerite we also say: "Gentle Lord, all that you did, for love of me and of the whole human race, leads me to love you, but the remembrance of your most holy Passion gives unequalled vigor to my power of affection to love you. That is why it seems to me that ... I have found what I so much desired: not to love anything other than you or in you or for love of you" (*ibid.*, *Meditazione* II, 46, p. 62).

At first glance this figure of a medieval Carthusian nun, as well as her life and her thought, seems distant from us, from our life, from our way of thinking and acting. But if we look at the essential aspect of this life we see that it also affects us and that it would also become the essential aspect of our own existence.

We have heard that Marguerite considered the Lord as a book, she fixed her gaze on the Lord; she considered him a mirror in which her own conscience also appeared. And from this mirror light entered her soul. She let into her own being the word, the life of Christ and thus she was transformed; her conscience was enlightened, she found criteria and light and was cleansed. It is precisely this that we also need: to let the words, life and light of Christ enter our conscience so that it is enlightened, understands what is true and good and what is wrong; may our conscience be enlightened and cleansed. Rubbish is not only on different streets of the world. There is also rubbish in our consciences and in our souls. Only the light of the Lord, his strength and his love, cleanses us, purifies us, showing us the right path. Therefore let us follow holy Marguerite in this gaze fixed on Jesus. Let us read the book of his life, let us allow ourselves to be enlightened and cleansed, to learn the true life.

CHAPTER NINE

St. Juliana of Cornillon[1]

This saint I now introduce is little known but the Church is deeply indebted to her, not only because of the holiness of her life but also because, with her great fervor, she contributed to the institution of one of the most important solemn Liturgies of the year: *Corpus Christi*.

She is St. Juliana de Cornillon, also known as St. Juliana of Liège. We know several facts about her life, mainly from a biography that was probably written by a contemporary cleric; it is a collection of various testimonies of people who were directly acquainted with the saint.

Juliana was born near Liège, Belgium, between 1191 and 1192. It is important to emphasize this place because at that time the Diocese of Liège was, so to speak, a true "Eucharistic Upper Room." Before Juliana, eminent theologians had illustrated the supreme value of the Sacrament of the Eucharist and, again in Liège, there were groups of women generously dedicated to Eucharistic worship and to fervent communion. Guided by exemplary priests, they lived together, devoting themselves to prayer and to charitable works.

---

[1] Pope Benedict XVI, General Audience, November 17, 2010.

Orphaned at the age of five, Juliana, together with her sister Agnes, was entrusted to the care of the Augustinian nuns at the convent and leprosarium of Mont-Cornillon. She was taught mainly by a sister called "Sapienza" [wisdom], who was in charge of her spiritual development to the time Juliana received the religious habit and thus became an Augustinian nun.

She became so learned that she could read the words of the Church Fathers, of St. Augustine and St. Bernard in particular, in Latin. In addition to a keen intelligence, Juliana showed a special propensity for contemplation from the outset. She had a profound sense of Christ's presence, which she experienced by living the Sacrament of the Eucharist especially intensely and by pausing frequently to meditate upon Jesus' words: "And lo, I am with you always, to the close of the age" (Mt 28:20).

When Juliana was sixteen she had her first vision which recurred subsequently several times during her Eucharistic adoration. Her vision presented the moon in its full splendor, crossed diametrically by a dark stripe. The Lord made her understand the meaning of what had appeared to her. The moon symbolized the life of the Church on earth, the opaque line, on the other hand, represented the absence of a liturgical feast for whose institution Juliana was asked to plead effectively: namely, a feast in which believers would be able to adore the Eucharist so as to increase in faith, to advance in the practice of the virtues and to make reparation for offenses to the Most Holy Sacrament.

Juliana, who in the meantime had become Prioress of the convent, kept this revelation that had filled her heart with joy a secret for about twenty years. She then confided it to two other fervent adorers of the Eucharist, Blessed Eva, who lived as a hermit, and Isabella, who had joined her at the Monastery of Mont-Cornillon. The three women established a sort of "spiritual alliance" for the purpose of glorifying the Most Holy Sacrament.

They also chose to involve a highly regarded priest, John of Lausanne, who was a canon of the Church of St. Martin in Liège. They asked him to consult theologians and clerics on what was important to them. Their affirmative response was encouraging.

What happened to Juliana of Cornillon occurs frequently in the lives of saints. To have confirmation that an inspiration comes from God it is always necessary to be immersed in prayer, to wait patiently, to seek friendship and exchanges with other good souls and to submit all things to the judgment of the Pastors of the Church.

It was in fact Bishop Robert Torote of Liège who, after initial hesitation, accepted the proposal of Juliana and her companions and first introduced the Solemnity of *Corpus Christi* in his diocese. Later other bishops following his example instituted this Feast in the territories entrusted to their pastoral care.

However, to increase their faith the Lord often asks saints to sustain trials. This also happened to Juliana who had to bear the harsh opposition of certain members of the clergy and even of the superior on whom her monastery depended.

Of her own free will, therefore, Juliana left the Convent of Mont-Cornillon with several companions. For ten years — from 1248 to 1258 — she stayed as a guest at various monasteries of Cistercian sisters. She edified all with her humility, she had no words of criticism or reproach for her adversaries and continued zealously to spread Eucharistic worship.

She died at Fosses-La-Ville, Belgium, in 1258. In the cell where she lay the Blessed Sacrament was exposed and, according to her biographer's account, Juliana died contemplating with a last effusion to love Jesus in the Eucharist whom she had always loved, honored and adored. Jacques Pantaléon of Troyes was also won over to the good cause of the Feast of *Corpus Christi* during his ministry as Archdeacon in Liège. It was he who, having become Pope with the name of Urban IV in 1264, instituted the Solemnity of *Corpus Christi* on the Thursday after Pentecost as a feast of precept for the universal Church.

In the Bull of its institution, entitled *Transiturus de hoc mundo* (August 11, 1264), Pope Urban even referred discreetly to Juliana's mystical experiences, corroborating their authenticity. He wrote: "Although the Eucharist is celebrated solemnly every day, we deem it fitting that at least once a year it be celebrated with greater honor and a solemn commemoration.

"Indeed we grasp the other things we commemorate with our spirit and our mind, but this does not mean that we obtain their real presence. On the contrary, in this sacramental commemoration of Christ, even though in a different form, Jesus Christ is present with us in his own substance. While he was about to ascend into Heaven he said, 'And lo, I am with you always, to the close of the age' (Matthew 28:20)."

Jesus Christ is present with us in his own substance.

The Pontiff made a point of setting an example by celebrating the solemnity of *Corpus Christi* in Orvieto, the town where he was then residing. Indeed, he ordered that the famous *Corporal* with the traces of the Eucharistic miracle which had occurred in Bolsena the previous year, 1263, be kept in Orvieto Cathedral — where it still is today. In this miracle, a priest was consecrating the bread and the wine when he was overcome by strong doubts about the Real Presence of the Body and Blood of Christ in the Sacrament of the Eucharist. A few drops of blood began miraculously to ooze from the consecrated Host, thereby confirming what our faith professes.

Urban IV asked one of the greatest theologians of history, St. Thomas Aquinas — who at that time was accompanying the Pope and was in Orvieto — to compose the texts of the Liturgical Office for this great feast. They are masterpieces, still in use in the Church today, in which theology and poetry are fused. These texts pluck at the heartstrings in an expression of praise and gratitude to the Most Holy Sacrament, while the mind, penetrating the mystery with wonder, recognizes in the Eucharist the Living and Real Presence of Jesus, of his

Sacrifice of love that reconciles us with the Father, and gives us salvation.

Although after the death of Urban IV the celebration of the Feast of *Corpus Christi* was limited to certain regions of France, Germany, Hungary and Northern Italy, it was another Pontiff, John XXII, who in 1317 re-established it for the universal Church. Since then the Feast experienced a wonderful development and is still deeply appreciated by the Christian people.

I would like to affirm with joy that today there is a "Eucharistic springtime" in the Church: How many people pause in silence before the Tabernacle to engage in a loving conversation with Jesus! It is comforting to know that many groups of young people have rediscovered the beauty of praying in adoration before the Most Blessed Sacrament.

I am thinking, for example, of our Eucharistic adoration in Hyde Park, London. I pray that this Eucharistic "springtime" may spread increasingly in every parish and in particular in Belgium, St. Juliana's homeland.

Bl. John Paul II said in his Encyclical *Ecclesia de Eucharistia*: "In many places, adoration of the Blessed Sacrament is also an important daily practice and becomes an inexhaustible source of holiness. The devout participation of the faithful in the Eucharistic procession on the Solemnity of the Body and Blood of Christ is a grace from the Lord which yearly brings joy to those who take part in it. Other positive signs of Eucharistic faith and love might also be mentioned" (n. 10).

In remembering St. Juliana of Cornillon let us also re-new our faith in the Real Presence of Christ in the Eucharist. As we are taught by the *Compendium of the Catechism of the Catholic Church,* "Jesus Christ is present in the Eucharist in a unique and incomparable way. He is present in a true, real and substantial way, with his Body and his Blood, with his Soul and his Divinity. In the Eucharist, therefore, there is present in a sacramental way, that is, under the Eucharistic Species of bread and wine, Christ whole and entire, God and Man" (n. 282).

Dear friends, fidelity to the encounter with the Christ in the Eucharist in Holy Mass on Sunday is essential for the journey of faith, but let us also seek to pay frequent visits to the Lord present in the Tabernacle! In gazing in adoration at the consecrated Host, we discover the gift of God's love, we discover Jesus' Passion and Cross and likewise his Resurrection. It is precisely through our gazing in adoration that the Lord draws us towards him into his mystery in order to transform us as he transforms the bread and the wine.

The saints never failed to find strength, consolation and joy in the Eucharistic encounter. Let us repeat before the Lord present in the Most Blessed Sacrament the words of the Eucharistic hymn "*Adoro te devote*": [Devoutly I adore Thee]: Make me believe ever more in you, "Draw me deeply into faith, / Into Your hope, into Your love."

CHAPTER TEN

St. Catherine of Siena[1]

A woman who played an eminent role in the history of the Church was St. Catherine of Siena. The century in which she lived — the fourteenth — was a troubled period in the life of the Church and throughout the social context of Italy and Europe. Yet, even in the most difficult times, the Lord does not cease to bless his people, bringing forth saints who give a jolt to minds and hearts, provoking conversion and renewal.

Catherine is one of these and still today speaks to us and impels us to walk courageously toward holiness to be ever more fully disciples of the Lord.

Born in Siena in 1347, into a very large family, she died in Rome in 1380. When Catherine was sixteen years old, motivated by a vision of St. Dominic, she entered the Third Order of the Dominicans, the female branch known as the *Mantellate*. While living at home, she confirmed her vow of virginity made privately when she was still an adolescent and dedicated herself to prayer, penance, and works of charity, especially for the benefit of the sick.

When the fame of her holiness spread, she became the protagonist of an intense activity of spiritual guidance

---

[1] Pope Benedict XVI, General Audience, November 24, 2010.

for people from every walk of life: nobles and politicians, artists and ordinary people, consecrated men and women and religious, including Pope Gregory XI who was living at Avignon in that period and whom she energetically and effectively urged to return to Rome.

She traveled widely to press for the internal reform of the Church and to foster peace among the States. It was also for this reason that Bl. Pope John Paul II chose to declare her Co-Patroness of Europe: may the Old Continent never forget the Christian roots that are at the origin of its progress and continue to draw from the Gospel the fundamental values that assure justice and harmony.

Like many of the saints, Catherine knew great suffering. Some even thought that they should not trust her, to the point that in 1374, six years before her death, the General Chapter of the Dominicans summoned her to Florence to interrogate her. They appointed Raymund of Capua, a learned and humble Friar and a future Master General of the Order, as her spiritual guide. Having become her confessor and also her "spiritual son," he wrote a first complete biography of the saint. She was canonized in 1461.

The teaching of Catherine, who learned to read with difficulty and learned to write in adulthood, is contained in the *Dialogue of Divine Providence* or *Libro della Divina Dottrina*, a masterpiece of spiritual literature, in her *Epistolario* and in the collection of her *Prayers*.

Her teaching is endowed with such excellence that in 1970 the Servant of God Paul VI declared her a Doctor of the Church, a title that was added to those of Co-Patroness of the City of Rome — at the wish of Bl. Pius IX — and of Patroness of Italy — in accordance with the decision of Venerable Pius XII.

In a vision that was ever present in Catherine's heart and mind Our Lady presented her to Jesus who gave her a splendid ring, saying to her: "I, your Creator and Savior, espouse you in the faith, that you will keep ever pure until you celebrate your eternal nuptials with me in Heaven" (Bl. Raimondo da Capua, *S. Caterina da Siena, Legenda maior*, n. 115, Siena, 1998). This ring was visible to her alone. In this extraordinary episode we see the vital center of Catherine's religious sense, and of all authentic spirituality: Christocentrism. For her Christ was like the spouse with whom a relationship of intimacy, communion, and faithfulness exists; he was the best beloved whom she loved above any other good. This profound union with the Lord is illustrated by another episode in the life of this outstanding mystic: the exchange of hearts. According to Raymond of Capua who passed on the confidences Catherine received, the Lord Jesus appeared to her "holding in his holy hands a human heart, bright red and shining." He opened her side and put the heart within her saying: "Dearest daughter, as I took your heart away from you the other day, now, you see, I am giving you mine, so that you can go on living with it forever" (*ibid.*). Catherine truly lived St. Paul's words, "It is no longer I who live, but Christ who lives in me" (Gal 2:20).

Like the Sienese saint, every believer feels the need to be conformed with the sentiments of the heart of Christ to love God and his neighbor as Christ himself loves. And we can all let our hearts be transformed and learn to love like Christ in a familiarity with him that is nourished by prayer, by meditation on the Word of God, and by the sacraments, above all by receiving Holy Communion frequently and with devotion. Catherine also belongs to the throng of saints devoted to the Eucharist with which I concluded my Apostolic Exhortation *Sacramentum Caritatis* (*cf.* n. 94). Dear brothers and sisters, the Eucharist is an extraordinary gift of love that God continually renews to nourish our journey of faith, to strengthen our hope, and to inflame our charity, to make us more and more like him.

A true and authentic spiritual family was built up around such a strong and genuine personality; people fascinated by the moral authority of this young woman with a most exalted lifestyle were at times also impressed by the mystical phenomena they witnessed, such as her frequent ecstasies. Many put themselves at Catherine's service and above all considered it a privilege to receive spiritual guidance from her. They called her "mother" because, as her spiritual children, they drew spiritual nourishment from her. Today too the Church receives great benefit from the exercise of spiritual motherhood by so many women, lay and consecrated, who nourish souls with thoughts of God, who strengthen the people's faith and direct Christian life towards ever loftier peaks. "Son, I say to you and call you," Catherine wrote to one of her spiritual sons, Giovanni Sabbatini, a Carthusian, "inasmuch as I give birth to you in continuous prayers and desire in the presence of God, just as a mother gives birth to a son" (*Epistolario, Lettera* n. 141: To *Fr. Giovanni de' Sabbatini*). She would usually address the Dominican Fr. Bartolomeo de Dominici with these words: "Most beloved and very dear brother and son in Christ sweet Jesus."

Another trait of Catherine's spirituality is linked to the gift of tears. They express an exquisite, profound sensitivity, a capacity for being moved and for tenderness. Many saints have had the gift of tears, renewing the emotion of Jesus himself who did not hold back or hide his tears at the tomb of his friend Lazarus and at the grief of Mary and Martha or at the sight of Jerusalem during his last days on this earth. According to Catherine, the tears of saints are mingled with the blood of Christ, of which she spoke in vibrant tones and with symbolic images that

According to Catherine, the tears of saints are mingled with the blood of Christ.

were very effective: "Remember Christ crucified, God and man.... Make your aim the Crucified Christ, hide in the wounds of the Crucified Christ and drown in the blood of the Crucified Christ" (*Epistolario, Lettera* n. 16: *Ad uno il cui nome si tace* [to one who remains anonymous]). Here we can understand why, despite her awareness of the human shortcomings of priests, Catherine always felt very great reverence for them: through the sacraments and the Word they dispense the saving power of Christ's Blood. The Sienese saint always invited the sacred ministers, including the Pope whom she called "sweet Christ on earth," to be faithful to their responsibilities, motivated always and only by her profound and constant love of the Church. She said before she died: "In leaving my body, truly I have consumed and given my life in the Church and for the Holy Church, which is for me a most unique grace" (*Raimondo da Capua, S. Caterina da Siena, Legenda maior*, n. 363). Hence we learn from St. Catherine the most sublime science: to know and love Jesus Christ and his Church. In the Dialogue of Divine Providence, she describes Christ, with an unusual image, as a bridge flung between Heaven and earth. This bridge consists of three great stairways constituted by the feet, the side, and the mouth of Jesus. Rising by these stairways the soul passes through the three stages of every path to sanctification: detachment from sin; the practice of the virtues and of love; sweet and loving union with God.

Dear brothers and sisters, let us learn from St. Catherine to love Christ and the Church with courage, intensely and sincerely. Therefore let us make our own St. Catherine's words that we read in the *Dialogue of Divine Providence* at the end of the chapter that speaks of Christ as a bridge: "Out of mercy you have washed us in his Blood, out of mercy you have wished to converse with creatures. O crazed with love! It did not suffice for you to take flesh, but you also wished to die!... O mercy! My heart drowns in thinking of you: for no matter where I turn to think, I find only mercy" (chapter 30, pp. 79-80).

CHAPTER ELEVEN

Julian of Norwich [1]

I still remember with great joy the Apostolic Journey I made in the United Kingdom in September of 2010. England is a land that has given birth to a great many distinguished figures who enhanced Church history with their testimony and their teaching. One of them, venerated both in the Catholic Church and in the Anglican Communion, is the mystic Julian of Norwich.

The — very scant — information on her life in our possession comes mainly from her *Revelations of Divine Love in Sixteen Showings*, the book in which this kindly and devout woman set down the content of her visions.

It is known that she lived from 1342 until about 1430, turbulent years both for the Church, torn by the schism that followed the Pope's return to Rome from Avignon, and for the life of the people who were suffering the consequences of a long drawn-out war between the kingdoms of England and of France. God, however, even in periods of tribulation, does not cease to inspire figures such as Julian of Norwich, to recall people to peace, love, and joy.

---

[1] Pope Benedict XVI, General Audience, December 1, 2010.

As Julian herself recounts, in May 1373, most likely on the thirteenth of that month, she was suddenly stricken with a very serious illness that in three days seemed to be carrying her to the grave. After the priest, who hastened to her bedside, had shown her the Crucified One, not only did Julian rapidly recover her health but she received the sixteen revelations that she subsequently wrote down and commented on in her book, *Revelations of Divine Love.*

And it was the Lord himself, fifteen years after these extraordinary events, who revealed to her the meaning of those visions. "'Would you learn to see clearly your Lord's meaning in this thing? Learn it well: Love was his meaning. Who showed it to you? Love.... Why did he show it to you? For Love'.... Thus I was taught that Love was our Lord's meaning" (Julian of Norwich, *Revelations of Divine Love,* Chapter 86).

Inspired by divine love, Julian made a radical decision. Like an ancient anchoress, she decided to live in a cell located near the church called after St. Julian, in the city of Norwich — in her time an important urban center not far from London.

She may have taken the name of Julian precisely from that saint to whom was dedicated the church in whose vicinity she lived for so many years, until her death.

This decision to live as a "recluse," the term in her day, might surprise or even perplex us. But she was not the only one to make such a choice. In those centuries a considerable number of women opted for this form of life, adopting rules specially drawn up, for them, such as the rule compiled by St. Aelred of Rievaulx.

The anchoresses, or "recluses," in their cells, devoted themselves to prayer, meditation, and study. In this way they developed a highly refined human and religious sensitivity which earned them the veneration of the people. Men and women of every age and condition in need of advice and comfort would devoutly seek them. It was not, therefore, an individualistic choice; precisely with this closeness to the Lord, Julian developed the ability to be a counselor to a great many people and to help those who were going through difficulties in this life.

We also know that Julian too received frequent visitors, as is attested by the autobiography of another fervent Christian of her time, Margery Kempe, who went to Norwich in 1413 to receive advice on her spiritual life. This is why, in her lifetime, Julian was called "Dame Julian," as is engraved on the funeral monument that contains her remains. She had become a mother to many.

Men and women who withdraw to live in God's company acquire by making this decision a great sense of compassion for the suffering and weakness of others. As friends of God, they have at their disposal a wisdom that the world — from which they have distanced themselves — does not possess and they amiably share it with those who knock at their door.

I therefore recall with admiration and gratitude the women's and men's cloistered monasteries. Today more than ever they are oases of peace and hope, a precious treasure for the whole Church, especially since they recall the primacy of God and the importance, for the journey of faith, of constant and intense prayer.

It was precisely in the solitude infused with God that Julian of Norwich wrote her *Revelations of Divine Love*. Two versions have come down to us, one that is shorter, probably the older, and one that is longer. This book contains a message of optimism based on the certainty of being loved by God and of being protected by his Providence.

In this book we read the following wonderful words: "And I saw full surely that ere God made us he loved us; which love was never lacking nor ever shall be. And in this love he has made all his works; and in this love he has made all things profitable to us; and in this love our life is everlasting ... in which love we have our beginning. And all this shall we see in God, without end" (*Revelations of Divine Love*, Chapter 86).

The theme of divine love recurs frequently in the visions of Julian of Norwich.

The theme of divine love recurs frequently in the visions of Julian of Norwich who, with a certain daring, did not hesitate to compare them also to motherly love. This is one of the most characteristic messages of her mystical theology.

The tenderness, concern, and gentleness of God's kindness to us are so great that they remind us, pilgrims on earth, of a mother's love for her children. In fact the biblical prophets also sometimes used this language that calls to mind the tenderness, intensity, and totality of God's love, which is manifested in creation and in the whole history of salvation that is crowned by the Incarnation of the Son.

God, however, always excels all human love, as the Prophet Isaiah says: "Can a woman forget her sucking child, that she should have no compassion on the son of her womb? Even these may forget, yet I will never forget you" (Is 49:15).

Julian of Norwich understood the central message for spiritual life: God is love, and it is only if one opens oneself to this love, totally and with total trust, and lets it become one's sole guide in life, that all things are transfigured, true peace and true joy found and one is able to radiate it.

I would like to emphasize another point. The *Catechism of the Catholic Church* cites the words of Julian of Norwich when it explains the viewpoint of the Catholic faith on an argument that never ceases to be a provocation to all believers (*cf.* nn. 304-313, 314).

If God is supremely good and wise, why do evil and the suffering of innocents exist? And the saints themselves asked this very question. Illumined by faith, they give an answer that opens our hearts to trust and hope: in the mysterious designs of Providence, God can draw a greater good even from evil, as Julian of Norwich wrote: "Here I was taught by the grace of God that I should steadfastly hold me in the Faith ... and that ... I should take my stand on and earnestly believe in ... that 'all manner of thing shall be well'" (*The Revelations of Divine Love,* Chapter 32).

Yes, dear brothers and sisters, God's promises are ever greater than our expectations. If we present to God, to his immense love, the purest and deepest desires of our heart, we shall never be disappointed. "And all will be well," "all manner of things shall be well": this is the final message that Julian of Norwich transmits to us and that I am also proposing to you today.

CHAPTER TWELVE

St. Veronica Giuliani[1]

This chapter is about a mystic who did not live in the Middle Ages. She is St. Veronica Giuliani, a Poor Clare Capuchin nun. December 27, 2010, was the three hundred fiftieth anniversary of her birth. Città di Castello, the place where she lived the longest and where she died, as well as Mercatello — her birthplace — and the Diocese of Urbino are celebrating this event with joy.

Indeed, Veronica was born on December 27, 1660, in Mercatello, in the Metauro Valley to Francesco Giuliani and Benedetta Mancini. She was the last of seven sisters, three of whom were to embrace the monastic life.

She was given the name "Orsola" [Ursula]. She was seven years old when her mother died and her father moved to Piacenza as customs superintendent of the Duchy of Parma. It was in this city that Ursula felt a growing desire to dedicate her life to Christ. The call to her became ever more pressing so that, when she was seventeen, she entered the strict cloister of the monastery of Capuchin Poor Clares in Città di Castello. She was to remain here for the rest of her life. Here she received the name of "Veronica,"

---

[1] Pope Benedict XVI, General Audience, December 15, 2010.

which means "true image" and she was in fact to become a true image of the Crucified Christ.

A year later she made her solemn religious profession and the process of configuration to Christ began for her, through much penance, great suffering, and several mystic experiences linked to the Passion of Jesus: being crowned with thorns, the mystical espousal, the wound in her heart and the stigmata.

In 1716, when she was fifty-six, she became Abbess of the monastery. She was reconfirmed in this office until her death in 1727, after a very painful prolonged agony that lasted thirty-three days and culminated in a joy so profound that her last words were: "I have found Love, Love has let himself be seen! This is the cause of my suffering. Tell everyone about it, tell everyone!" (*Summarium Beatificationis,* 115-120).

On July 9 she left her earthly dwelling place for the encounter with God. She was sixty-seven years old; fifty of those years she spent in the monastery of Città di Castello. She was canonized on May 26, 1839, by Pope Gregory XVI.

Veronica Giuliani wrote prolifically: letters, autobiographical reports, poems. However, the main source for reconstructing her thought is her *Diary*, which she began in 1693: about 22,000 handwritten pages that cover a span of thirty-four years of cloistered life.

Her writing flows spontaneously and continuously. There are no crossings-out, corrections, or punctuation marks in it, nor was the material divided into chapters or parts according to a plan.

Veronica did not intend to compose a literary work; on the contrary, Fr. Girolamo Bastianelli, a Filippini religious, in agreement with the diocesan Bishop Antonio Eustachi, obliged her to set down her experiences in writing.

St. Veronica has a markedly Christological and spousal spirituality: she experienced being loved by Christ, her faithful and sincere Bridegroom, to whom she wished to respond with an ever more involved and passionate love. She interpreted everything in the key of love and this imbued her with deep serenity. She lived everything in union with Christ, for love of him, and with the joy of being able to demonstrate to him all the love of which a creature is capable. The Christ to whom Veronica was profoundly united was the suffering Christ of the Passion, death and Resurrection; it was Jesus in the act of offering himself to the Father in order to save us.

Her intense and suffering love for the Church likewise stemmed from this experience, in its dual form of prayer and offering. The saint lived in this perspective: she prayed, suffered and sought "holy poverty," as one "dispossessed," and the loss of self (*cf. ibid.*, III, 523), precisely in order to be like Christ who gave the whole of himself.

In every page of her writings Veronica commends someone to the Lord, reinforcing her prayers of intercession with the offering of herself in every form of suffering. Her heart dilated to embrace all "the needs of the Holy Church," living anxiously the desire for the salvation of "the whole world" (*ibid.*, III-IV, *passim*). Veronica cried: "O sinners ... all men and all women, come to Jesus' heart; come to be cleansed by his most precious blood....He awaits you with open arms to embrace you" (*ibid.*, II, 16-17).

Motivated by ardent love, she gave her sisters in the monastery attention, understanding and forgiveness. She offered her prayers and sacrifices for the Pope, for her bishop, for priests and for all those in need, including the souls in purgatory.

She summed up her contemplative mission in these words: "We cannot go about the world preaching to convert souls but are bound to pray ceaselessly for all those souls who are offending God... particularly with our sufferings, that is, with a principle of crucified life" (*ibid.*, IV, 877). Our saint conceived this mission as "being in the midst" of men and God, of sinners and the Crucified Christ.

Veronica lived profound participation in the suffering love of Jesus, certain that "to suffer with joy" is the "key to love" (cf. *ibid.*, I, 299.417; III, 330.303.871; IV, 192). She emphasizes that Jesus suffers for humanity's sins, but also for the suffering that his faithful servants would have to endure down the centuries, in the time of the Church, precisely because of their solid and consistent faith.

She wrote: "His Eternal Father made them see and feel the extent of all the suffering that his chosen ones would have to endure, the souls dearest to him, that is, those who would benefit from his Blood and from all his sufferings" (*ibid.*, II, 170).

As the Apostle Paul says of himself: "Now I rejoice in my sufferings for your sake, and in my flesh I complete what is lacking in Christ's afflictions for the sake of his Body, that is, the Church" (Col 1:24).

Veronica reached the point of asking Jesus to allow her to be crucified with him. "In an instant," she wrote, "I saw five radiant rays issue from his most holy wounds; and they all shone on my face. And I saw these rays become, as it were, little tongues of fire. In four of them were the nails; and in one was the spear, as of gold, red hot and white hot: and it went straight through my heart, from one side to the other ... and the nails pierced my hands and feet. I felt great pain but in this same pain I saw myself, I felt myself totally transformed into God" (*Diary,* I, 897).

The saint was convinced that she was already participating in the Kingdom of God, but at the same time she invoked all the Saints of the Blessed Homeland to come to her aid on the earthly journey of her self-giving while she waited for eternal beatitude; this was her undying aspiration throughout her life (*cf. ibid.,* II, 909; V, 246).

With regard to the preaching of that time which often focused on "saving one's soul" in individual terms, Veronica shows a strong "sense of solidarity," a sense of communion with all her brothers and sisters on their way towards heaven and she lives, prays and suffers for all. The penultimate, earthly things, although appreciated in the Franciscan sense as gifts of the Creator, were always relative, altogether subordinate to "God's taste" and under the sign of radical poverty.

In the *communio sanctorum,* she explains the gift of herself to the Church, as the relationship between the pilgrim Church and the heavenly Church. "All the Saints," she wrote, "are up there thanks to the merit and the Passion of Jesus; but they cooperated with all that the Lord did, so that their life was totally ordered ... regulated by these same works (his)" (*ibid.*, III, 203).

We find many biblical citations in Veronica's writings, at times indirectly, but always precise. She shows familiarity with the Sacred Text, by which her spiritual experience was nourished. Furthermore, it should be pointed out that the intense moments of Veronica's mystical experience are never separate from the salvific events celebrated in the Liturgy, where the proclamation of the Word of God and listening to it has a special place. Hence, Sacred Scripture illumines, purifies, and confirms Veronica's experience, rendering it ecclesial. On the other hand, however, her experience itself, anchored in Sacred Scripture with uncommon intensity, guides one to a more profound and "spiritual" reading of the text itself, to enter into its hidden depths. Not only does she express herself with the words of Sacred Scripture but she also really lives by them, they take on life in her.

Hence, Sacred Scripture illumines, purifies, and confirms Veronica's experience, rendering it ecclesial.

For example, our saint often quotes the words of the Apostle Paul: "If God is for us, who is against us?" (Rom 8:31; *cf. Diary*, I, 714; II 116.1021; III, 48).

The assimilation of this Pauline text, her great trust and profound joy, becomes a *fait accompli* within her. "My soul," she wrote, "was bound to the divine will and I was truly established and fixed for ever in the will of God. It seemed to me that I should never again have to be separated from this will of God and I came to myself with these precise words: nothing will be able to separate me from the will of God, neither anxieties, nor sorrows nor toil nor contempt nor temptation nor creatures nor demons nor darkness, not even death itself, because, in life and in death, I want all, and in all things, the will of God" (*Diary*, IV, 272). Thus we have the certainty that death is not the last word, we are *fixed* in God's will, hence, truly, in eternal life.

In particular, Veronica proved a courageous witness of the beauty and power of Divine Love which attracted her, pervaded her and inflamed her. Crucified Love was impressed within her flesh as it was in that of St. Francis of Assisi, with Jesus' stigmata. "'My Bride,' the Crucified Christ whispers to me, 'the penance you do for those who suffer my disgrace is dear to me.'... Then detaching one of his arms from the Cross he made a sign to me to draw near to his side ... and I found myself in the arms of the Crucified One. What I felt at that point I cannot describe: I should have liked to remain forever in his most holy side" (*ibid.*, I, 37). This is also an image of her spiritual journey, of her interior life: to be in the embrace of the Crucified One and thus to remain in Christ's love for others.

Veronica also experienced a relationship of profound intimacy with the Virgin Mary, attested by the words she heard Our Lady say one day, which she reports in her *Diary*: "I made you rest on my breast, you were united with my soul, and from it you were taken as in flight to God" (IV, 901).

St. Veronica Giuliani invites us to develop, in our Christian life, our union with the Lord in living for others, abandoning ourselves to his will with complete and total trust, and the union with the Church, the Bride of Christ.

She invites us to participate in the suffering love of Jesus Crucified for the salvation of all sinners; she invites us to fix our gaze on Heaven, the destination of our earthly journey, where we shall live together with so many brothers and sisters the joy of full communion with God; she invites us to nourish ourselves daily with the Word of God, to warm our hearts and give our lives direction. The saint's last words can be considered the synthesis of her passionate mystical experience: *"I have found Love, Love has let himself be seen!"*

CHAPTER THIRTEEN

St. Catherine of Bologna[1]

In a previous chapter I spoke of St. Catherine of Siena. Now I would like to present to you another less well known saint who has the same name: St. Catherine of Bologna, a very erudite yet very humble woman. She was dedicated to prayer but was always ready to serve; generous in sacrifice but full of joy in welcoming Christ with the Cross.

Catherine was born in Bologna on September 8, 1413, the eldest child of Benvenuta Mammolini and John de' Vigri, a rich and cultured patrician of Ferrara, a doctor in law and a public lector in Padua, where he carried out diplomatic missions for Nicholas III d'Este, Marquis of Ferrara.

Not much information about Catherine's infancy and childhood is available and not all of it is reliable. As a child she lived in her grandparents' house in Bologna, where she was brought up by relatives, especially by her mother who was a woman of deep faith.

With her, Catherine moved to Ferrara when she was about ten years old and entered the court of Nicholas III d'Este as lady-in-waiting to Margaret, Nicholas' illegitimate daughter. The Marquis was transforming Ferrara

---

[1] Pope Benedict XVI, General Audience, December 29, 2010.

into a fine city, summoning artists and scholars from various countries. He encouraged culture and, although his private life was not exemplary, took great care of the spiritual good, moral conduct and education of his subjects.

In Ferrara Catherine was unaware of the negative aspects that are often part and parcel of court life. She enjoyed Margaret's friendship and became her confidante. She developed her culture by studying music, painting and dancing; she learned to write poetry and literary compositions and to play the viola; she became expert in the art of miniature painting and copying; she perfected her knowledge of Latin.

In her future monastic life she was to put to good use the cultural and artistic heritage she had acquired in these years. She learned with ease, enthusiasm and tenacity. She showed great prudence, as well as an unusual modesty, grace and kindness in her behavior.

However, one absolutely clear trait distinguished her: her spirit, constantly focused on the things of heaven. In 1427, when she was only fourteen years old and subsequent to certain family events, Catherine decided to leave the court to join a group of young noble women who lived a community life dedicating themselves to God. Her mother trustingly consented in spite of having other plans for her daughter.

We know nothing of Catherine's spiritual path prior to this decision. Speaking in the third person, she states that she entered God's service, "illumined by divine grace ... with an upright conscience and great fervor," attentive to holy prayer by night and by day, striving to acquire all the virtues she saw in others, "not out of envy but the better to please God in whom she had placed all her love" (*Le sette armi necessarie alla battaglia spirituali,* [The seven spiritual weapons], VII, 8, Bologna 1998, p. 12).

She made considerable spiritual progress in this new phase of her life but her trials, her inner suffering and especially the temptations of the devil were great and terrible. She passed through a profound spiritual crisis and came to the brink of despair (*cf. ibid.,* VII, 2, pp. 12-29). She lived in the night of the spirit, and was also deeply shaken by the temptation of disbelief in the Eucharist.

After so much suffering, the Lord comforted her: he gave her, in a vision, a clear awareness of the Real Presence in the Eucharist, an awareness so dazzling that Catherine was unable to express it in words (*cf. ibid.,* VIII, 2. pp. 42-46).

In this same period a sorrowful trial afflicted the community: tension arose between those who wished to follow the Augustinian spirituality and those who had more of an inclination for Franciscan spirituality.

Between 1429 and 1430, Lucia Mascheroni, in charge of the group, decided to found an Augustinian monastery. Catherine, on the other hand, chose with others to bind herself to the Rule of St. Clare of Assisi. It was a gift of Providence, because the community dwelled in the vicinity of the Church of the Holy Spirit, annexed to the convent of the Friars Minor who had adhered to the movement of the Observance.

Thus Catherine and her companions could take part regularly in liturgical celebrations and receive adequate spiritual assistance. They also had the joy of listening to the preaching of St. Bernardine of Siena (*cf. ibid.*, VII, 62, p. 26). Catherine recounts that in 1429 — the third year since her conversion — she went to make her confession to one of the Friars Minor whom she esteemed, she made a good Confession and prayed the Lord intensely to grant her forgiveness for all her sins and the suffering connected with them.

In a vision God revealed to her that he had forgiven her everything. It was a very strong experience of divine mercy which left an indelible mark upon her, giving her a fresh impetus to respond generously to God's immense love (*cf. ibid.* IX, 2, pp. 46-48).

In 1431 she had a vision of the Last Judgment. The terrifying spectacle of the damned impelled her to redouble her prayers and penance for the salvation of sinners. The devil continued to assail her and she entrusted herself ever more totally to the Lord and to the Virgin Mary (*cf. ibid.*, X, 3, pp. 53-54).

In her writings, Catherine has left us a few essential notes concerning this mysterious battle from which, with God's grace, she emerged victorious. She did so in order to instruct her sisters and those who intend to set out on the path of perfection: she wanted to put them on their guard against the temptations of the devil who often conceals himself behind deceptive guises, later to sow doubts about faith, vocational uncertainty and sensuality.

In her autobiographical and didactic treatise, *The Seven Spiritual Weapons,* Catherine offers in this regard teaching of deep wisdom and profound discernment. She speaks in the third person in reporting the extraordinary graces which the Lord gives to her and in the first person in confessing her sins. From her writing transpires the purity of her faith in God, her profound humility, the simplicity of her heart, her missionary zeal, her passion for the salvation of souls. She identifies seven weapons in the fight against evil, against the devil:

1. always to be careful and diligently strive to do good;
2. to believe that alone we will never be able to do something truly good;
3. to trust in God and, for love of him, never to fear in the battle against evil, either in the world or within ourselves;
4. to meditate often on the events and words of the life of Jesus, and especially on his Passion and his death;
5. to remember that we must die;
6. to focus our minds firmly on memory of the goods of Heaven;
7. to be familiar with Sacred Scripture, always cherishing it in our hearts so that it may give direction to all our thoughts and all our actions.

A splendid program of spiritual life, today too, for each one of us!

In the convent Catherine, in spite of being accustomed to the court in Ferrara, served in the offices of laundress, dressmaker and bread-maker and even looked after the animals. She did everything, even the lowliest tasks, with love and ready obedience, offering her sisters a luminous witness. Indeed she saw disobedience as that spiritual pride which destroys every other virtue. Out of obedience she accepted the office of novice mistress, although she considered herself unfit for this office, and God continued to inspire her with his presence and his gifts: in fact she proved to be a wise and appreciated mistress.

She did everything, even the lowliest tasks, with love and ready obedience.

Later the service of the parlor was entrusted to her. She found it trying to have to interrupt her prayers frequently in order to respond to those who came to the monastery grill, but this time too, the Lord did not fail to visit her and to be close to her. With her the monastery became an increasingly prayerful place of self-giving, of silence, of endeavor and of joy.

Upon the death of the abbess, the superiors thought immediately of her, but Catherine urged them to turn to the Poor Clares of Mantua who were better instructed in the Constitutions and in religious observance.

Nevertheless, a few years later, in 1456, she was asked at her monastery to open a new foundation in Bologna. Catherine would have preferred to end her days in Ferrara, but the Lord appeared to her and exhorted her to do God's will by going to Bologna as abbess. She prepared herself for the new commitment with fasting, scourging and penance.

She went to Bologna with eighteen sisters. As superior she set the example in prayer and in service; she lived in deep humility and poverty. At the end of her three-year term as abbess she was glad to be replaced but after a year she was obliged to resume her office because the newly elected abbess became blind. Although she was suffering and was afflicted with serious ailments that tormented her, she carried out her service with generosity and dedication.

For another year she urged her sisters to an evangelical life, to patience and constancy in trial, to fraternal love, to union with the divine Bridegroom, Jesus, so as to prepare her dowry for the eternal nuptials. It was a dowry that Catherine saw as knowing how to share the sufferings of Christ, serenely facing hardship, apprehension, contempt and misunderstanding (*cf. Le sette armi spirituali,* X, 20, pp. 57-58).

At the beginning of 1463 her health deteriorated. For the last time she gathered the sisters in Chapter, to announce her death to them and to recommend the observance of the Rule. Towards the end of February she was harrowed by terrible suffering that was never to leave her, yet despite her pain it was she who comforted her sisters, assuring them that she would also help them from heaven.

After receiving the Last Sacraments, she gave her confessor the text she had written: *The Seven Spiritual Weapons,* and entered her agony; her face grew beautiful and translucent; she still looked lovingly at those who surrounded her and died gently, repeating three times the name of Jesus. It was March 9, 1463 (*cf.* I. Bembo, *Specchio di illuminazione, Vita di S. Caterina a Bologna,* Florence 2001, chap. III). Catherine was to be canonized by Pope Clement XI on May 22, 1712. Her incorrupt body is preserved in the city of Bologna, in the chapel of the monastery of Corpus Domini.

Dear friends, with her words and with her life, St. Catherine of Bologna is a pressing invitation to let ourselves always be guided by God, to do his will daily, even if it often does not correspond with our plans, to trust in his Providence which never leaves us on our own. In this perspective, St. Catherine speaks to us; from the distance of so many centuries she is still very modern and speaks to our lives.

She, like us, suffered temptations; she suffered the temptations of disbelief, of sensuality, of a difficult spiritual struggle. She felt forsaken by God, she found herself in the darkness of faith. Yet in all these situations she was always holding the Lord's hand, she did not leave him, she did not abandon him. And walking hand in hand with the Lord, she walked on the right path and found the way of light.

So it is that she also tells us: take heart, even in the night of faith, even amidst our many doubts, do not let go of the Lord's hand, walk hand in hand with him; believe in God's goodness. This is how to follow the right path!

And I would like to stress another aspect: her great humility. She was a person who did not want to be someone or something; she did not care for appearances, she did not want to govern. She wanted to serve, to do God's will, to be at the service of others. And for this very reason Catherine was credible in her authority, because she was able to see that for her authority meant, precisely, serving others.

Let us ask God, through the intercession of our saint, for the gift to achieve courageously and generously the project he has for us, so that he alone may be the firm rock on which our lives are built.

CHAPTER FOURTEEN

St. Catherine of Genoa[1]

After Catherine of Siena and Catherine of Bologna, now I would like to speak about another saint: Catherine of Genoa, known above all for her vision of purgatory. The text that describes her life and thought was published in this Ligurian city in 1551. It is in three sections: her *Vita* [Life], properly speaking, the *Dimostratione et dechiaratione del purgatorio* — better known as *Treatise on purgatory* — and her *Dialogo tra l'anima e il corpo* (cf. *Libro de la Vita mirabile et dottrina santa, de la beata Caterinetta da Genoa. Nel quale si contiene una utile et catholica dimostratione et dechiaratione del purgatorio*, Genoa 1551). The final version was written by Catherine's confessor, Fr. Cattaneo Marabotto.

Catherine was born in Genoa in 1447. She was the youngest of five. Her father, Giacomo Fieschi, died when she was very young. Her mother, Francesca di Negro, provided such an effective Christian education that the elder of her two daughters became a religious.

When Catherine was sixteen, she was given in marriage to Giuliano Adorno, a man who after various trading

---

[1] Pope Benedict XVI, General Audience, January 12, 2011.

and military experiences in the Middle East had returned to Genoa in order to marry.

Married life was far from easy for Catherine, partly because of the character of her husband who was given to gambling. Catherine herself was at first induced to lead a worldly sort of life in which, however, she failed to find serenity. After ten years, her heart was heavy with a deep sense of emptiness and bitterness.

A unique experience on March 20, 1473, sparked her conversion. She had gone to the Church of San Benedetto in the monastery of Nostra Signora delle Grazie [Our Lady of Grace], to make her confession and, kneeling before the priest, "received," as she herself wrote, "a wound in my heart from God's immense love." It came with such a clear vision of her own wretchedness and shortcomings and at the same time of God's goodness that she almost fainted.

Her heart was moved by this knowledge of herself — knowledge of the empty life she was leading and of the goodness of God. This experience prompted the decision that gave direction to her whole life. She expressed it in the words: "no longer the world, no longer sin" (cf. *Vita Mirabile*, 3rv). Catherine did not stay to make her Confession.

On arriving home she entered the remotest room and spent a long time weeping. At that moment she received an inner instruction on prayer and became aware of God's immense love for her, a sinner. It was a spiritual experience she had no words to describe (cf. *Vita Mirabile*, 4r).

It was on this occasion that the suffering Jesus appeared to her, bent beneath the Cross, as he is often portrayed in the saint's iconography. A few days later she returned to the priest to make a good confession at last. It was here that began the "life of purification" which for many years caused her to feel constant sorrow for the sins she had committed and which spurred her to impose forms of penance and sacrifice upon herself, in order to show her love to God.

On this journey Catherine became ever closer to the Lord until she attained what is called "unitive life," namely, a relationship of profound union with God.

In her Vita it is written that her soul was guided and instructed from within solely by the sweet love of God which gave her all she needed. Catherine surrendered herself so totally into the hands of the Lord that she lived, for about twenty-five years, as she wrote, "without the assistance of any creature, taught and governed by God alone" (*Vita*, 117r-118r), nourished above all by constant prayer and by Holy Communion which she received every day, an unusual practice in her time. Only many years later did the Lord give her a priest who cared for her soul.

Catherine was always reluctant to confide and reveal her experience of mystical communion with God, especially because of the deep humility she felt before the Lord's graces. The prospect of glorifying him and of being able to contribute to the spiritual journey of others alone spurred her to recount what had taken place within her, from the moment of her conversion, which is her original and fundamental experience.

The place of her ascent to mystical peaks was Pammatone Hospital, the largest hospital complex in Genoa, of which she was director and animator. Hence Catherine lived a totally active existence despite the depth of her inner life. In Pammatone a group of followers, disciples and collaborators formed around her, fascinated by her life of faith and her charity. Indeed her husband, Giuliano Adorno, was so won over that he gave up his dissipated life, became a Third Order Franciscan and moved into the hospital to help his wife.

Catherine's dedication to caring for the sick continued until the end of her earthly life on September 15, 1510. From her conversion until her death there were no extraordinary events but two elements characterize her entire life: on the one hand her mystical experience, that is, the profound union with God, which she felt as spousal union, and on the other, assistance to the sick, the organization of the hospital and service to her neighbor, especially the neediest and the most forsaken. These two poles, God and neighbor, totally filled her life, virtually all of which she spent within the hospital walls.

Dear friends, we must never forget that the more we love God and the more constantly we pray, the better we will succeed in truly loving those who surround us, who are close to us, so that we can see in every person the Face of the Lord whose love knows no bounds and makes no distinctions. The mystic does not create distance from others or an abstract life, but rather approaches other people so that they may begin to see and act with God's eyes and heart.

Catherine's thought on purgatory, for which she is particularly well known, is summed up in the last two parts of the book mentioned above: The *Treatise on purgatory* and the *Dialogues between the body and the soul*. It is important to note that Catherine, in her mystical experience, never received specific revelations on purgatory or on the souls being purified there. Yet, in the writings inspired by our saint, purgatory is a central element and the description of it has characteristics that were original in her time.

The first original passage concerns the "place" of the purification of souls. In her day it was depicted mainly using images linked to space: a certain space was conceived of in which purgatory was supposed to be located.

Catherine, however, did not see purgatory as a scene in the bowels of the earth: for her it is not an exterior but rather an interior fire. This is purgatory: an inner fire. The saint speaks of the Soul's journey of purification on the way to full communion with God, starting from her own experience of profound sorrow for the sins committed, in comparison with God's infinite love (cf. *Vita Mirabile*, 171v).

The saint speaks of the Soul's journey of purification on the way to full communion with God.

We heard of the moment of conversion when Catherine suddenly became aware of God's goodness, of the infinite distance of her own life from this goodness and of a burning fire within her. And this is the fire that purifies, the interior fire of purgatory. Here too is an original feature in comparison with the thought of her time.

In fact, she does not start with the afterlife in order to recount the torments of purgatory — as was the custom in her time and perhaps still is today — and then to point out the way to purification or conversion. Rather our saint begins with the inner experience of her own life on the way to Eternity.

"The soul," Catherine says, "presents itself to God still bound to the desires and suffering that derive from sin and this makes it impossible for it to enjoy the beatific vision of God." Catherine asserts that God is so pure and holy that a soul stained by sin cannot be in the presence of the divine majesty (cf. *Vita Mirabile*, 177r).

We too feel how distant we are, how full we are of so many things that we cannot see God. The soul is aware of the immense love and perfect justice of God and consequently suffers for having failed to respond in a correct and perfect way to this love; and love for God itself becomes a flame, love itself cleanses it from the residue of sin.

In Catherine we can make out the presence of theological and mystical sources on which it was normal to draw in her time. In particular, we find an image typical of Dionysius the Areopagite: the thread of gold that links the human heart to God himself. When God purified man, he bound him with the finest golden thread, that is, his love, and draws him toward himself with such strong affection that man is as it were "overcome and won over and completely beside himself."

Thus man's heart is pervaded by God's love that becomes the one guide, the one driving force of his life (cf. *Vita Mirabile*, 246rv). This situation of being uplifted towards God and of surrender to his will, expressed in the image of the thread, is used by Catherine to express the action of divine light on the souls in purgatory, a light that purifies and raises them to the splendor of the shining radiance of God (cf. *Vita Mirabile*, 179r).

Dear friends, in their experience of union with God, saints attain such a profound knowledge of the divine mysteries in which love and knowledge interpenetrate, that they are of help to theologians themselves in their commitment to study, to *intelligentia fidei*, to an *intelligentia* of the mysteries of faith, to attain a really deeper knowledge of the mysteries of faith, for example, of what purgatory is.

With her life St. Catherine teaches us that the more we love God and enter into intimacy with him in prayer the more he makes himself known to us, setting our hearts on fire with his love. In writing about purgatory, the saint reminds us of a fundamental truth of faith that becomes for us an invitation to pray for the deceased so that they may attain the beatific vision of God in the Communion of Saints (cf. *Catechism of the Catholic Church*, n. 1032).

Moreover the humble, faithful and generous service in Pammatone Hospital that the saint rendered throughout her life is a shining example of charity for all and an encouragement, especially for women who, with their precious work enriched by their sensitivity and attention to the poorest and neediest, make a fundamental contribution to society and to the Church.

CHAPTER FIFTEEN

St. Joan of Arc[1]

Joan of Arc was a young saint who lived at the end of the Middle Ages who died at the age of nineteen, in 1431. This French saint, mentioned several times in the *Catechism of the Catholic Church*, is particularly close to St. Catherine of Siena, Patroness of Italy and of Europe, of whom I spoke in a previous chapter. They were in fact two young women of the people, lay women consecrated in virginity, two committed mystics, not in the cloister, but in the midst of the most dramatic reality of the Church and the world of their time. They are perhaps the most representative of those "strong women" who, at the end of the Middle Ages, fearlessly bore the great light of the Gospel in the complex events of history. We could liken them to the holy women who stayed on Calvary, close to the Crucified Jesus and to Mary his Mother, while the Apostles had fled and Peter himself had denied him three times.

The Church in that period was going through the profound crisis of the great schism of the West, which lasted almost forty years. In 1380, when Catherine of Siena died, there was not only a Pope but also an antipope; when

---

[1] Pope Benedict XVI, General Audience, January 26, 2011.

Joan was born, in 1412, there was a Pope as well as two antipopes. In addition to this internal laceration in the Church, were the continuous fratricidal wars among the Christian peoples of Europe, the most dramatic of which was the protracted Hundred Years' War between France and England.

Joan of Arc did not know how to read or write, but the depths of her soul can be known thanks to two sources of exceptional historical value: the two *Trials* that concern her. The first, the *Trial of Condemnation* (*PCon*), contains the transcription of the long and numerous interrogations to which Joan was subjected in the last months of her life (February-May 1431) and reports the saint's own words. The second, the *Trial of Nullity of the Condemnation* or of "rehabilitation" (*PNul*), contains the depositions of about one hundred twenty eyewitnesses of all the periods of her life (*cf. Procès de Condamnation de Jeanne d'Arc*, 3 vol. and *Procès en Nullité de la Condamnation de Jeanne d'Arc*, 5 vol., ed. Klincksieck, Paris, 1960-1989).

Joan was born at Domremy, a little village on the border between France and Lorraine. Her parents were well-off peasants, known to all as good Christians. From them she received a sound religious upbringing, considerably influenced by the spirituality of the *Name of Jesus*, taught by St. Bernardine of Siena and spread in Europe by the Franciscans.

The *Name of Mary* was always associated with the Name of Jesus and thus, against the background of popular piety, Joan's spirituality was profoundly Christocentric and Marian. From childhood, she showed great love and compassion for the poorest, the sick, and all the suffering, in the dramatic context of the war.

We know from Joan's own words that her religious life developed as a mystical experience from the time when she was thirteen (*PCon,* I, p. 47-48). Through the "voice" of St. Michael the Archangel, Joan felt called by the Lord to intensify her Christian life and also to commit herself in person to the liberation of her people. Her immediate response, her "yes," was her vow of virginity, with a new commitment to sacramental life and to prayer: daily participation in Mass, frequent Confession and Communion, and long periods of silent prayer before the Crucified One or the image of Our Lady.

The young French peasant girl's compassion and dedication in the face of her people's suffering were intensified by her mystical relationship with God. One of the most original aspects of this young woman's holiness was precisely this link between mystical experience and political mission. The years of her hidden life and her interior development were followed by the brief but intense two years of her public life: a year of *action* and a year of *passion.*

At the beginning of 1429, Joan began her work of liberation. The many witnesses show us this young woman, who was only seventeen years old, as a very strong and determined person, able to convince people who felt insecure and discouraged. Overcoming all obstacles, she met the Dauphin of France, the future King Charles VII, who subjected her to an examination in Poitiers by some theologians of the university. Their opinion was positive: they saw in her nothing evil, only a good Christian.

On March 22, 1429, Joan dictated an important letter to the King of England and to his men at arms who were besieging the city of Orléans (*ibid.*, pp. 221-222). Hers was a true proposal of peace in justice between the two Christian peoples in light of the Names of Jesus and Mary, but it was rejected, and Joan had to gird herself to fight for the city's liberation which took place on May 8. The other culminating moment of her political action was the coronation of King Charles VII in Rheims on July 17, 1429. For a whole year, Joan lived with the soldiers, carrying out among them a true mission of evangelization. Many of them testified to her goodness, her courage, and her extraordinary purity. She was called by all and by herself "La pucelle" ("the Maid"), that is, virgin.

Joan's *passion* began on May 23, 1430, when she fell into enemy hands and was taken prisoner. On December 23 she was led to the city of Rouen. There the long and dramatic *Trial of Condemnation* took place that began in February 1431 and ended on May 30 with her being burned at the stake.

It was a great and solemn Trial, at which two ecclesiastical judges presided, Bishop Pierre Cauchon and the Inquisitor Jean le Maistre, but in fact it was conducted entirely by a large group of theologians from the renowned University of Paris, who took part in the Trial as assessors. They were French clerics, who, on the side politically opposed to Joan's, had *a priori* a negative opinion of both her and her mission. This trial is a distressing page in the history of holiness and also an illuminating page on the mystery of the Church which, according to the words of the Second Vatican Council, is "at once holy and always in need of purification" (*Lumen Gentium,* n. 8).

The Trial was the dramatic encounter between this saint and her judges, who were clerics. Joan was accused and convicted by them, even condemned as a heretic and sent to the terrible death of being burned at the stake. Unlike the holy theologians who had illuminated the University of Paris, such as St. Bonaventure, St. Thomas Aquinas, and Bl. Duns Scotus, of whom I have spoken in several catecheses, these judges were theologians who lacked charity and the humility to see God's action in this young woman.

The words of Jesus, who said that God's mysteries are revealed to those who have a child's heart while they remain hidden to the learned and the wise who have no humility (*cf.* Lk 10:21), spring to mind. Thus, Joan's judges were radically incapable of understanding her or of perceiving the beauty of her soul. They did not know that they were condemning a saint.

Joan's appeal to the Pope, on May 24, was rejected by the tribunal. On the morning of May 30, in prison, she received Holy Communion for the last time and was immediately led to her torture in the Old Market Square. She asked one of the priests to hold up a processional Cross in front of the stake. Thus she died, her gaze fixed upon the Crucified Jesus and crying out several times the Name of Jesus (*PNul*, I, p. 457; *cf. Catechism of the Catholic Church*, n. 435). About twenty-five years later the *Trial of Nullity*, which opened under the authority of Pope Calixtus III, ended with a solemn sentence that declared the condemnation null and void (July 7, 1456; *PNul*, II, pp. 604-610). This long trial, which collected the evidence of witnesses and the opinions of many theologians, all favorable to Joan, sheds light on her innocence and on her perfect fidelity to the Church. Joan of Arc was subsequently canonized by Benedict XV in 1920.

Dear brothers and sisters, the *Name of Jesus,* invoked by our saint until the very last moments of her earthly life was like the continuous breathing of her soul, like the beating of her heart, the center of her whole life. *The Mystery of the Charity of Joan of Arc* which so fascinated the poet Charles Péguy was this total love for Jesus and for her neighbor in Jesus and for Jesus. This saint had understood that Love embraces the whole of the reality of God and of the human being, of heaven and of earth, of the Church and of the world. Jesus always had pride of place in her life, in accordance to her beautiful affirmation: "We must serve God first" (*PCon*, I, p. 288; *cf. Catechismo della Chiesa Cattolica*, n. 223). Loving him means always doing his will. She declared with total surrender and trust: "I entrust myself to God my Creator, I love him with my whole my heart" (*PCon*, I, p. 337).

> *Jesus always had pride of place in her life, in accordance to her beautiful affirmation: "We must serve God first."*

With the vow of virginity, Joan consecrated her whole being exclusively to the one Love of Jesus: "it was the promise that she made to Our Lord to preserve the virginity of her body and her mind well" (*PCon*, I, pp. 149-150).

Virginity of soul is the *state of grace*, a supreme value, for her more precious than life. It is a gift of God which is to be received and preserved with humility and trust. One of the best known texts of the first *Trial* concerns precisely this: "Asked if she knew that she was in God's grace, she replied: 'If I am not, may it please God to put me in it; if I am, may it please God to keep me there'" (*ibid.*, p. 62; *cf. Catechism of the Catholic Church*, n. 2005).

Our saint lived prayer in the form of a continuous dialogue with the Lord who also illuminated her dialogue with the judges and gave her peace and security. She asked him with trust: "Sweetest God, in honor of your holy Passion, I ask you, if you love me, to show me how I must answer these men of the Church" (*PCon, I*, p. 252). Joan saw Jesus as the "King of Heaven and of the earth." She therefore had painted on her standard the image of "Our Lord holding the world" (*ibid.*, p. 172): the emblem of her political mission. The liberation of her people was a work of human justice which Joan carried out in charity, for love of Jesus. Her holiness is a beautiful example for lay people engaged in politics, especially in the most difficult situations. Faith is the light that guides every decision, as a century later another great saint, the Englishman Thomas More, was to testify.

In Jesus Joan contemplated the whole reality of the Church, the "Church triumphant" of Heaven, as well as the "Church militant" on earth. According to her words, "About Jesus Christ and the Church, I simply know they're just one thing" (*ibid.*, p. 166). This affirmation, cited in the *Catechism of the Catholic Church* (n. 795), has a truly heroic character in the context of the *Trial of Condemnation*, before her judges, men of the Church who were persecuting and condemning her. In the Love of Jesus Joan found the strength to love the Church to the very end, even at the moment she was sentenced.

I like to recall that St. Joan of Arc had a profound influence on a young saint of the modern age: Thérèse of the Child Jesus. In the context of a completely different life, spent in the cloister, the Carmelite of Lisieux felt very close to Joan, living in the heart of the Church and participating in Christ's suffering for the world's salvation. The Church has brought them together as Patronesses of France, after the Virgin Mary.

St. Thérèse expressed her desire to die, like Joan, with the Name of Jesus on her lips (*Manoscritto B,* 3r), and she was motivated by the same great love for Jesus and her neighbor, lived in consecrated virginity.

Dear brothers and sisters, with her luminous witness St. Joan of Arc invites us to a high standard of Christian living: to make prayer the guiding motive of our days; to have full trust in doing God's will, whatever it may be; to live charity without favoritism, without limits and drawing, like her, from the Love of Jesus a profound love for the Church.

CHAPTER SIXTEEN

St. Teresa of Ávila[1]

In the course of previous catecheses that I have chosen to dedicate to the Fathers of the Church and to great theologians and women of the Middle Ages, I have also had the opportunity to reflect on certain saints proclaimed Doctors of the Church on account of the eminence of their teaching.

Continuing with my presentation on the Doctors of the Church, I now would like to present a saint who is one of the peaks of Christian spirituality of all time — St. Teresa of Ávila [also known as St. Teresa of Jesus].

St. Teresa, whose name was Teresa de Cepeda y Ahumada, was born in Ávila, Spain, in 1515. In her autobiography she mentions some details of her childhood: she was born into a large family, which included her "father and mother, who were devout and feared God." She had three sisters and nine brothers.

While she was still a child, and not yet nine years old, she had the opportunity to read the lives of several martyrs, which inspired in her such a longing for martyrdom that she briefly ran away from home in order to die a mar-

---

[1] Pope Benedict XVI, General Audience, February 2, 2011.

tyr's death and to go to heaven (cf. *Vida*, [*Life*], 1, 4); "I want to see God," the little girl told her parents.

A few years later Teresa was to speak of her childhood reading and to state that she had discovered in it the way of truth which she sums up in two fundamental principles.

On the one hand was the fact that "all things of this world will pass away" while on the other God alone is "for ever, ever, ever," a topic that recurs in her best known poem: "Let nothing disturb you, Let nothing frighten you, All things are passing away: God never changes. Patience obtains all things. Whoever has God lacks nothing; God alone suffices." She was about twelve years old when her mother died, and she implored the Virgin Most Holy to be her mother (cf. *Vida*, I, 7).

If in her adolescence the reading of profane books had led to the distractions of a worldly life, her experience as a pupil of the Augustinian nuns of Santa María de las Gracias de Ávila and her reading of spiritual books, especially the classics of Franciscan spirituality, introduced her to recollection and prayer.

When she was twenty she entered the Carmelite Monastery of the Incarnation, also in Ávila. In her religious life she took the name "Teresa of Jesus." Three years later she fell seriously ill, so ill that she remained in a coma for four days, looking as if she were dead (cf. *Vida*, 5, 9).

In the fight against her own illnesses too the Saint saw the combat against weaknesses and the resistance to God's call: "I wished to live," she wrote, "but I saw clearly that I was not living, but rather wrestling with the shadow of death; there was no one to give me life, and I was not able to take it. He who could have given it to me had good reasons for not coming to my aid, seeing that he had brought me back to himself so many times, and I as often had left him" (*Vida*, 7, 8).

In 1543 she lost the closeness of her relatives; her father died and all her siblings, one after another, emigrated to America. In Lent 1554, when she was 39 years old, Teresa reached the climax of her struggle against her own weaknesses. The fortuitous discovery of the statue of "a Christ most grievously wounded," left a deep mark on her life (*cf. Vida*, 9).

The saint, who in that period felt deeply in tune with the St. Augustine of the *Confessions*, thus describes the decisive day of her mystical experience: "and... a feeling of the presence of God would come over me unexpectedly, so that I could in no wise doubt either that he was within me, or that I was wholly absorbed in him" (*Vida*, 10, 1).

Parallel to her inner development, the saint began in practice to realize her ideal of the reform of the Carmelite Order: in 1562 she founded the first reformed Carmel in Ávila, with the support of the city's Bishop, Don Alvaro de Mendoza, and shortly afterwards also received the approval of John Baptist Rossi, the Order's Superior General.

In the years that followed, she continued her foundations of new Carmelite convents, seventeen in all. Her meeting with St. John of the Cross was fundamental. With him, in 1568, she set up the first convent of Discalced Carmelites in Duruelo, not far from Ávila.

In 1580 she obtained from Rome the authorization for her reformed Carmels as a separate, autonomous Province. This was the starting point for the Discalced Carmelite Order.

Indeed, Teresa's earthly life ended while she was in the middle of her founding activities. She died on the night of October 15, 1582, in Alba de Tormes, after setting up the Carmelite Convent in Burgos, while on her way back to Ávila. Her last humble words were: "After all I die as a child of the Church," and "O my Lord and my Spouse, the hour that I have longed for has come. It is time to meet one another."

Teresa spent her entire life for the whole Church although she spent it in Spain. She was beatified by Pope Paul V in 1614 and canonized by Gregory XV in 1622. The Servant of God Paul VI proclaimed her a "Doctor of the Church" in 1970.

Teresa of Jesus had no academic education but always set great store by the teachings of theologians, men of letters, and spiritual teachers. As a writer, she always adhered to what she had lived personally through or had seen in the experience of others (cf. *Prologue* to *The Way of Perfection*), in other words basing herself on her own first-hand knowledge.

Teresa had the opportunity to build up relations of spiritual friendship with many saints and with St. John of the Cross in particular. At the same time she nourished herself by reading the Fathers of the Church, St. Jerome, St. Gregory the Great, and St. Augustine.

Among her most important works we should mention first of all her autobiography, *El libro de la vida* (the book of life), which she called *Libro de las misericordias del Señor* [Book of the Lord's Mercies].

Written in the Carmelite Convent at Ávila in 1565, she describes the biographical and spiritual journey, as she herself says, to submit her soul to the discernment of the "Master of things spiritual," St. John of Ávila. Her purpose was to highlight the presence and action of the merciful God in her life. For this reason the work often cites her dialogue in prayer with the Lord. It makes fascinating reading because not only does the Saint recount that she is reliving the profound experience of her relationship with God but also demonstrates it.

In 1566, Teresa wrote *El Camino de Perfección* [The Way of Perfection]. She called it *Advertencias y consejos que da Teresa de Jesús a sus hermanas* [recommendations and advice that Teresa of Jesus offers to her sisters]. It was composed for the twelve novices of the Carmel of St. Joseph in Ávila. Teresa proposes to them an intense program of contemplative life at the service of the Church, at the root of which are the evangelical virtues and prayer.

Among the most precious passages is her commentary on the *Our Father,* as a model for prayer. St. Teresa's most famous mystical work is *El Castillo interior* [The Interior Castle]. She wrote it in 1577 when she was in her prime.

It is a reinterpretation of her own spiritual journey and, at the same time, a codification of the possible development of Christian life towards its fullness, holiness, under the action of the Holy Spirit.

Teresa refers to the structure of a castle with seven rooms as an image of human interiority.

Teresa refers to the structure of a castle with seven rooms as an image of human interiority. She simultaneously introduces the symbol of the silkworm reborn as a butterfly, in order to express the passage from the natural to the supernatural.

The Saint draws inspiration from Sacred Scripture, particularly the Song of Songs, for the final symbol of the "Bride and Bridegroom" which enables her to describe, in the seventh room, the four crowning aspects of Christian life: the Trinitarian, the Christological, the anthropological, and the ecclesial.

St. Teresa devoted the *Libro de la fundaciones* [Book of the Foundations], which she wrote between 1573 and 1582, to her activity as foundress of the reformed Carmels. In this book she speaks of the life of the nascent religious group. This account, like her autobiography, was written above all in order to give prominence to God's action in the work of founding new monasteries.

It is far from easy to sum up in a few words Teresa's profound and articulate spirituality. I would like to mention a few essential points. In the first place St. Teresa proposes the evangelical virtues as the basis of all Christian and human life and, in particular, detachment from possessions, that is, evangelical poverty, and this concerns all of us; love for one another as an essential element of community and social life; humility as love for the truth; determination as a fruit of Christian daring; theological hope, which she describes as the thirst for living water. Then we should not forget the human virtues: affability, truthfulness, modesty, courtesy, cheerfulness, culture.

Secondly, St. Teresa proposes a profound harmony with the great biblical figures and eager listening to the Word of God. She feels above all closely in tune with the Bride in the Song of Songs and with the Apostle Paul, as well as with Christ in the Passion and with Jesus in the Eucharist. The saint then stresses how essential prayer is. Praying, she says, "means being on terms of friendship with God frequently conversing in secret with him who, we know, loves us" (*Vida* 8, 5). St. Teresa's idea coincides with Thomas Aquinas' definition of theological charity as "amicitia quaedam hominis ad Deum," a type of human friendship with God, who offered humanity his friendship first; it is from God that the initiative comes (*cf. Summa Theologiae* II-II, 23, 1).

Prayer is life and develops gradually, in pace with the growth of Christian life: it begins with vocal prayer, passes through interiorization by means of meditation and recollection, until it attains the union of love with Christ and with the Holy Trinity. Obviously, in the development of prayer climbing to the highest steps does not mean abandoning the previous type of prayer. Rather, it is a gradual deepening of the relationship with God that envelops the whole of life.

Rather than a pedagogy, Teresa's is a true "mystagogy" of prayer: she teaches those who read her works how to pray by praying with them. Indeed, she often interrupts her account or exposition with a prayerful outburst.

Another subject dear to the saint is the centrality of Christ's humanity. For Teresa, in fact, Christian life is the personal relationship with Jesus that culminates in union with him through grace, love, and imitation. Hence the importance she attaches to meditation on the Passion and on the Eucharist as the presence of Christ in the Church for the life of every believer, and as the heart of the Liturgy. St. Teresa lives out unconditional love for the Church: she shows a lively *"sensus Ecclesiae,"* in the face of the episodes of division and conflict in the Church of her time.

She reformed the Carmelite Order with the intention of serving and defending the "Holy Roman Catholic Church," and was willing to give her life for the Church (*cf. Vida*, 33,5).

A final essential aspect of Teresian doctrine which I would like to emphasize is perfection, as the aspiration of the whole of Christian life and as its ultimate goal. The saint has a very clear idea of the "fullness" of Christ, re-lived by the Christian. At the end of the route through *The Interior Castle*, in the last "room," Teresa describes this fullness, achieved in the indwelling of the Trinity, in union with Christ through the mystery of his humanity.

Dear brothers and sisters, St. Teresa of Jesus is a true teacher of Christian life for the faithful of every time. In our society, which all too often lacks spiritual values, St. Teresa teaches us to be unflagging witnesses of God, of his presence and of his action. She teaches us truly to feel this thirst for God that exists in the depths of our hearts, this desire to see God, to seek God, to be in conversation with him and to be his friends.

This is the friendship we all need that we must seek anew, day after day. May the example of this saint, profoundly contemplative and effectively active, spur us, too, every day to dedicate the right time to prayer, to this openness to God, to this journey, in order to seek God, to see him, to discover his friendship and so to find true life; indeed many of us should truly say: "I am not alive, I am not truly alive because I do not live the essence of my life."

Therefore time devoted to prayer is not time wasted, it is time in which the path of life unfolds, the path unfolds to learning from God an ardent love for him, for his Church, and practical charity for our brothers and sisters.

CHAPTER SEVENTEEN

St. Thérèse of Lisieux[1]

St. Thérèse of Lisieux, Thérèse of the Child Jesus and of the Holy Face, lived in this world for only twenty-four years, at the end of the nineteenth century, leading a very simple and hidden life but, after her death and the publication of her writings, she became one of the best-known and best-loved saints. "Little Thérèse" has never stopped helping the simplest souls, the little, the poor, and the suffering who pray to her. However, she has also illumined the whole Church with her profound spiritual doctrine to the point that Bl. Pope John Paul II chose, in 1997, to give her the title "Doctor of the Church," in addition to that of Patroness of Missions, which Pius XI had already attributed to her in 1939. My beloved predecessor described her as an "expert in the *scientia amoris*" (*Novo Millennio Ineunte*, n. 42). Thérèse expressed this science, in which she saw the whole truth of the faith shine out in love, mainly in the *story of her life*, published a year after her death with the title *The Story of a Soul*. The book immediately met with enormous success, it was translated into many languages and disseminated throughout the world.

---

[1] Pope Benedict XVI, General Audience, April 6, 2011.

I would like to invite you to rediscover this small, but great, treasure, this luminous comment on the Gospel lived to the full! *The Story of a Soul*, in fact, is a marvelous *story of Love*, told with such authenticity, simplicity, and freshness that the reader cannot but be fascinated by it! But what was this Love that filled Thérèse's whole life, from childhood to death? Dear friends, this Love has a Face, it has a Name, it is Jesus! The saint speaks continuously of Jesus. Let us therefore review the important stages of her life, to enter into the heart of her teaching.

Thérèse was born on January 2, 1873, in Alençon, a city in Normandy, in France. She was the last daughter of Louis and Zélie Martin, a married couple and exemplary parents, who were beatified together on October 19, 2008. They had nine children, four of whom died at a tender age. Five daughters were left, who all became religious. Thérèse, at the age of four, was deeply upset by the death of her mother (Ms A 13r). Her father then moved with his daughters to the town of Lisieux, where the saint was to spend her whole life. Later Thérèse, affected by a serious nervous disorder, was healed by a divine grace which she herself described as the "smile of Our Lady" (*ibid.*, 29v-30v). She then received her First Communion, which was an intense experience (*ibid.*, 35r), and made Jesus in the Eucharist the center of her life.

The "Grace of Christmas" of 1886 marked the important turning-point, which she called her "complete conversion" (*ibid.*, 44v-45r). In fact she recovered totally from her childhood hyper-sensitivity and began "to run as a giant." At the age of fourteen, Thérèse became ever closer, with great faith, to the Crucified Jesus. She took to heart the apparently desperate case of a criminal sentenced to death who was impenitent. "I wanted at all costs to prevent him from going to hell," the saint wrote, convinced that her prayers would put him in touch with the redeeming Blood of Jesus. It was her first and fundamental experience of *spiritual motherhood*: "I had such great trust in the Infinite Mercy of Jesus," she wrote. Together with Mary Most Holy, young Thérèse loved, believed, and hoped with "a mother's heart" (cf. Pr 6/ior).

In November 1887, Thérèse went on pilgrimage to Rome with her father and her sister Céline (*ibid.*, 55v-67r). The culminating moment for her was the audience with Pope Leo XIII, whom she asked for permission to enter the Carmel of Lisieux when she was only fifteen. A year later her wish was granted. She became a Carmelite, "to save souls and to pray for priests" (*ibid.*, 69v).

At the same time, her father began to suffer from a painful and humiliating mental illness. It caused Thérèse great suffering which led her to contemplation of the Face of Jesus in his Passion (*ibid.*, 71rc). Thus, her name as a religious — *Sister Thérèse of the Child Jesus and of the Holy Face* — expresses the program of her whole life in communion with the central Mysteries of the Incarnation and the Redemption. Her religious profession, on the Feast of the Nativity of Mary, September 8, 1890, was a true spiritual espousal in evangelical "littleness," characterized by the symbol of the flower: "It was the Nativity of Mary.

What a beautiful feast on which to become the Spouse of Jesus! It was the *little* newborn Holy Virgin who presented her *little* Flower to the *little* Jesus" (*ibid.*, 77r).

For Thérèse, being a religious meant being a *bride of Jesus and a mother of souls* (cf. Ms B, 2v). On the same day, the saint wrote a prayer which expressed the entire orientation of her life: she asked Jesus for the gift of his infinite Love, to be the smallest, and above all she asked for the salvation of all human beings: "That no soul may be damned today" (Pr 2).

Of great importance is her *Offering to Merciful Love*, made on the Feast of the Most Holy Trinity in 1895 (Ms A, 83v-84r; Pr 6). It was an offering that Thérèse immediately shared with her sisters, since she was already acting novice mistress.

Ten years after the "Grace of Christmas" in 1896, came the "Grace of Easter," which opened the last period of Thérèse's life with the beginning of her passion in profound union with the Passion of Jesus. It was the passion of her body, with the illness that led to her death through great suffering, but it was especially the passion of the soul, with a very painful *trial of faith* (Ms C, 4v-7v). With Mary beside the Cross of Jesus, Thérèse then lived the most heroic faith, as a light in the darkness that invaded her soul. The Carmelite was aware that she was living this great trial for the salvation of all the atheists of the modern world, whom she called "brothers."

She then lived fraternal love even more intensely (8r-33v): for the sisters of her community, for her two spiritual missionary brothers, for the priests, and for all people, especially the most distant. She truly became a "universal sister"! Her lovable, smiling charity was the expression of the profound joy whose secret she reveals: "Jesus, my joy is loving you" (P 45/7). In this context of suffering, living the greatest love in the smallest things of daily life, the saint brought to fulfillment her vocation to be Love in the heart of the Church (cf. Ms B, 3v).

Thérèse died on the evening of September 30, 1897, saying the simple words, "My God, I love you!" looking at the Crucifix she held tightly in her hands. These last words of the saint are the key to her whole doctrine, to her interpretation of the Gospel; the act of love, expressed in her last breath was as it were the continuous breathing of her soul, the beating of her heart. The simple words "*Jesus I love you,*" are at the heart of all her writings. The act of love for Jesus immersed her in the Most Holy Trinity. She wrote: "Ah, you know, Divine Jesus, I love you / The spirit of Love enflames me with his fire, / It is in loving you that I attract the Father" (P 17/2).

Thérèse is one of the "little" ones of the Gospel who let themselves be led by God to the depths of his Mystery.

Dear friends, we too, with St. Thérèse of the Child Jesus, must be able to repeat to the Lord every day that we want to live of love for Him and for others, to learn at the school of the saints to love authentically and totally. Thérèse is one of the "little" ones of the Gospel who let themselves be led by God to the depths of his Mystery. A guide for all, especially those who, in the People of God, carry out their ministry as theologians. With humility and charity, faith, and hope, Thérèse continually entered the heart of Sacred Scripture which contains the Mystery of Christ. And this interpretation of the Bible, nourished by the *science of love*, is not in opposition to academic knowledge. The *science of the saints*, in fact, of which she herself speaks on the last page of her *The Story of a Soul*, is the loftiest science.

"All the saints have understood and in a special way perhaps those who fill the universe with the radiance of the evangelical doctrine. Was it not from prayer that St. Paul, St. Augustine, St. John of the Cross, St. Thomas Aquinas, Francis, Dominic, and so many other friends of God drew that *wonderful science* which has enthralled the loftiest minds?" (cf. Ms C 36r).

Inseparable from the Gospel, for Thérèse the Eucharist was the sacrament of Divine Love that stoops to the extreme to raise us to him. In her last *Letter*, on an image that represents Jesus the Child in the consecrated Host, the saint wrote these simple words: "I cannot fear a God who made himself so small for me! [...] I love him! In fact, he is nothing but Love and Mercy!" (LT 266).

In the Gospel Thérèse discovered above all the Mercy of Jesus, to the point that she said: "To me, He has given His Infinite Mercy, and it is in this ineffable mirror that I contemplate His other divine attributes. Therein all appear to me radiant with Love. His Justice, even more perhaps than the rest, seems to me to be clothed with Love" (Ms A, 84r).

In these words she expresses herself in the last lines of *The Story of a Soul*: "I have only to open the Holy Gospels and at once I breathe the perfume of Jesus' life, and then I know which way to run; and it is not to the first place, but to the last, that I hasten.... I feel that even had I on my conscience every crime one could commit ... my heart broken with sorrow, I would throw myself into the arms of my Savior Jesus, because I know that he loves the Prodigal Son who returns to him" (Ms C, 36v-37r).

"Trust and Love" are therefore the final point of the account of her life, two words, like beacons, that illumined the whole of her journey to holiness, to be able to guide others on the same "little way of trust and love," of spiritual childhood (cf. Ms C, 2v-3r; LT 226).

Trust, like that of the child who abandons himself in God's hands, inseparable from the strong, radical commitment of true love, which is the total gift of self forever, as the saint says, contemplating Mary: "Loving is giving all, and giving oneself" (*Why I love thee, Mary*, P 54/22). Thus Thérèse points out to us all that Christian life consists in living to the full the grace of Baptism in the total gift of self to the Love of the Father, in order to live like Christ, in the fire of the Holy Spirit, his same love for all the others.

Books by Pope Benedict XVI
from Our Sunday Visitor

The Apostles

The Fathers, Volume I
St. Clement to St. Augustine

The Fathers, Volume II
St. Leo to St. Bernard

The Apostles, Illustrated

The Fathers, Illustrated
Volume I – St. Clement to St. Paulinus of Nola
Volume II – St. Augustine to St. Maximus the Confessor

Breakfast with Benedict

Questions and Answers

Saint Paul the Apostle

The Virtues

Great Teachers

Our Sunday Visitor Publishing
1-800-348-2440 ◆ www.osv.com